Advance Blurbs
Living for a Higher Purpose

This publication by Titilola Vivour-Adeniyi is an acceptable rehash of the injunctions against sexual immoralities which have been handed down to humans from ages past, but the practice of which still persists even in this contemporary age.

The author has demonstrated that, with doggedness, it is possible to rise through the ranks in the public service. Having built a flourishing career in the legal profession, she has availed prospective readers her wealth of experience as a resource person in addressing the growing menace of domestic and gender-based violence plaguing modern societies with a view to dimming its preponderance.

Expectedly, readers can be drawn nearer to nature's standpoint and the readiness of the law as well to enforce sanity in the face of avoidable social misbehaviours. I recommend it to ALL!

– HRM Oba (Barr.) Semiudeen Orimadegun Kasali B.L. LL.M,
Adeboruwa of Igbogbo Kingdom.

Living for a Higher Purpose, is a revolutionary idea and an accurate documentation of an exemplary and selfless public service in the pursuit of common good for the majority of the people of Lagos State and by extension, Nigeria, particularly in the sensitive and life-saving field of Sexual and Gender Based Violence prevention.

This inspirational and priceless account is written by no other person than an eminently qualified public officer, who has over the years made an indelible mark in public service, walking the talk, leading by example, and employing selflessness as her watch word.

She is an example of a public servant, uncommon, rara avis, a Merchant of Hope indeed.

–Taiwo Akinlami, Global Contents Owner and Ethicist, The Securing A Friendly and Protective Environment® for Children Society (S.A.F.E®).

Addressing issues of domestic and sexual violence formed an important part of the Social Development and Security pillar of Governor Akinwunmi Ambode's administration. During my tenure as Attorney-General and Commissioner for Justice, priority was given to building the right foundation in safeguarding the wellbeing of survivors, and ensuring the justice system was well positioned to holding perpetrators fully accountable.

I am proud of Lola for demonstrating commitment, zeal and passion in fighting this good fight, and that she has been able to document the progress made in Lagos State's quest towards eradicating Sexual and Gender Based Violence.

I therefore whole heartedly recommend this book to everyone who is desirous of making indelible impact, particularly in public service.

- **Mr Adeniji Kazeem,** SAN, 17th Attorney-General and Commissioner for Justice, Lagos State.

The facts and narratives in *Living for a Higher Purpose*, shed light on how a vision for greater good can be nurtured to fruition through hard work, advocacy and a collaborative spirit. This book is worth having and reading again and again.

- Dr Sodipo Oluwajimi, Consultant Family Physician, Lagos State University Teaching Hospital (LASUTH).

One of the best practices for holistic survivors centred approach to SGBV is to establish a multi sectoral team made up of professionals that provide support services to survivors of rape and sexual violence. When members of the team work together, it reduces the trauma suffered by survivors which may lead to increase in prosecution. Lagos state government adopted this approach in a bid to provide an enabling environment for survivors to speak out and get needed help and support. In establishing the Domestic and Sexual Violence Response Team (DSVRT), the government brought together state agencies, civil society organisations and the media with a view to providing expedited response to domestic and sexual violence.

Considering the mutual distrust between government and civil society organisations, it required a special kind of coordination for the response team to achieve its purpose. It required a coordinator who did not only understand the challenges of this "unholy" alliance but also one who had needed skill sets to coordinate and manage the team in a way that did not make some members feel less important than others. Lola provided this coordination and management of the team. She was accessible and responsive not only to survivors who were the primary beneficiaries of the team, but also served as a liaison between the government and civil society members on the team.

The successful partnership between Mirabel Centre and the Lagos state government can be traced to Lola who recognised the important role the centre plays in providing support services to survivors thereby contributing to achieving the objectives of the Response Team. A public servant who is not a civil servant, Lola showed by example that commitment, passion and dedication can produce outstanding results in the face of daunting challenges of negative social norms, rape culture, weak institutions, culture of silence, etc. Lola took DSVRT to great heights, setting the standard for other states to copy. In her role as the Executive Secretary of the Domestic and Sexual Violence Agency, there is enough evidence that the agency will achieve the purpose for which it was set up.

– **Mrs Itoro Eze-ANABA**, founder, Mirabel Centre.

The book, *Living for a Higher Purpose – Inspiring Hope* through the Nigerian Public Service is a must-read for any person who wants renewed hope in the Nigerian dream. It could not have been written by a better author and is certainly coming at the best time for the country. The author started this journey as a young person and has through persistence, developed one of the most successful institutions in Nigeria in recent times. I recommend this book to all—students, professionals, development practitioners, government officials and patriots. The book shows that with integrity, thirst for knowledge, love for country and a lot of commitment, the possibilities are endless. It also makes a strong case for youth leadership for a new Nigeria.

- **Akingbolahan Adeniran**, Partner, Awodi & Co. (Legal Consultants)

LIVING FOR A HIGHER PURPOSE

Published in Nigeria in 2022 by Quramo Publishing
under its QLife imprint

The Simi Johnson Centre
13 Sinari Daranijo Street, Victoria Island
Lagos, Nigeria.
+234 01 454 7878
info@quramo.com
www.quramo.com

Cover Design by Darlington Sabali

A catalogue record of this book will be available from the National Library of Nigeria.

LIVING FOR A HIGHER PURPOSE

Inspiring Hope Through
The Nigerian Public Service

TITILOLA VIVOUR-ADENIYI

Life Q

CONTENTS

ACKNOWLEDGMENTS

I think the beginning is the first place to start. I want to thank God, my Creator for deeming me worthy to be the answer and solution to several people that I have been privileged to come in contact with. My sincere appreciation and gratitude go to my parents, Mr Olawale Rhodes-Vivour and Mrs Nkechinyere Rhodes-Vivour for investing their time, energy and resources in ensuring my brothers, my sister and I grew up with the right values. I appreciate my brothers; Gbadebo, Adeyemo, and Oluwatosin Rhodes-Vivour, and of course my sister, Ayodele Vivour-Osinaike for their unwavering support and encouragement over the years.

I must acknowledge the visionary leadership of the previous governors of Lagos State, His Excellency, Senator Bola Ahmed Tinubu; His Excellency, Mr Babatunde Raji Fashola (SAN), His Excellency, Mr Akinwunmi Ambode as well as the incumbent governor, Governor, Babajide SanwoOlu for demonstrating the political will to fight the menace of Sexual and Gender-Based Violence, and rid Lagos State of it. I also appreciate the First Lady of Lagos State, Dr Ibijoke Sanwo-Olu as well as the wife of the Deputy Governor of Lagos State, Her Excellency, Chief (Mrs.) Oluremi Hamzat for using their good offices to ensure certain barriers were overcome and giant strides were attained in just about two years due to a genuine interest in a worthy cause.

The Deputy Governors of Lagos State, Her Excellency, Princess Orelope Adefulire, Her Excellency, Dr Oluranti Adebule, as well as His Excellency, Dr Kadri Obafemi Hamzat, thank you for believing in the vision of making Lagos State free of all forms of sexual and gender-based violence.

I thank my first boss in Nigeria, Mrs Oyinkansola Badejo Okusanya, for laying the critical foundation for my journey into Public Service as well as Mr Olasupo Shasore, SAN, for helping to mould my work ethic and approach to governance. I am indebted to Mr Ade Ipaye for believing in me and giving me the opportunity to discover myself and flourish. I thank Mr Adeniji Kazeem, SAN, for believing in Domestic and Sexual Violence Response Team (DSVRT) and ensuring the DSVRT dream and vision was realised. I am also very grateful to Mr Moyosore Onigbanjo, SAN for believing in me as a person and believing in the vision of DSVRT. He is always eager to show me off. I have been privileged to work with four consecutive Attorneys General who have positively impacted the DSVRT vision; this I would never take for granted.

I use this opportunity to appreciate the Learned Solicitors-General I have been privileged to work with, Mr Lawal Pedro, SAN (for always lending us funds, especially as we did not have a budget during his tenure), Ms Funlola Odunlami, for her leadership and support through the years and of course, Ms Titilayo Shitta-Bey, a great amazon and mentor. Working with you has been seamless. Thank you very much.

I have been privileged to work with distinguished Commissioners of Police (CP), including CP Fatai Owoseni, CP Edgal, CP Muazu and CP Hakeem Odumosu. Distinguished police officers who understand that investigating and prosecuting Sexual and Gender- Based Violence requires trained, designated and dedicated personnel in the Lagos Police Command.

In Lagos, we have been privileged to have Chief Judges of the Lagos State Judiciary who demonstrate judicial activism; The Hon. Justice Opeyemi Oke, The Hon. Justice Kazeem Alogba. Profound appreciation is extended to My Lords for their commitment in ensuring justice for survivors.

I must at this juncture, appreciate esteemed traditional rulers who I have been privileged to work with, over the years. They include: His Royal Majesty, **Oba Kabiru Adewale Sotobi**, The Ayangburen of Ikorodu (Ilufemi Loba), His Royal Majesty, **Oba Semiudeen Orimadegun Kasali** (Emugoriade I) Adeboruwa of Igbogbo Kingdom, Igbogbo, His Royal Majesty, **Oba (Dr.) Sulaiman Adesina Raji Ashade I**, Oni Iba of Iba Kingdom, Iba, His Royal Majesty, **Oba Shefiu Olatunji Adewale**, The Olu of Epe, His Royal Highness, **Oba Kamoru Ishola Animashaun**, The Oloja of Epe. I remain grateful to Your Royal Majesties for ensuring Sexual and Gender Based Violence issues are swiftly and decisively addressed.

I would also like to use this opportunity to acknowledge members, particularly, pioneer members of the Lagos State Domestic and Sexual Violence Response Team: Mrs Omotilewa Ibirogba, (Director for Citizens' Rights), Hon. Justice Serifat Solebo (Lagos State Judiciary), Mr Akingbolahan Adeniran (Special Assistant to the Hon. Attorney-General), Mrs Omotola Rotimi (Director, Office of Public Defender), Late Mrs Kehinde Idowu (Child Protection Unit, Ministry of Youth and Social Development), Mrs Kehinde Oke (Family Social Services, Ministry of Youth and Social Development), Mrs Alaba Fadairo (Ministry of Women Affairs & Poverty Alleviation), Mrs Bola Akingbade, (Public Relations Officer, Ministry of Justice), Mr Bajulaiye (Directorate of Public Prosecutions), Dr Taiwo Johnson (Ministry of Health), Mrs Ibidunni Alakija-Ladapo (Ministry of Health), Mrs Busola Agagu (Ministry of Education), Mrs Itoro Eze-Anaba (Founder, Mirabel Centre), Mrs Bose Ironsi (Founder, Women's Rights and Health Project), Dr Keziah Awosika, (Lagos State Gender Advocacy Team), Mrs Olabisi Oghogho (State Accountability for Voice Initiative), Mrs Shola Soyele (Judiciary Correspondent, Channels TV), Mr Olaleye Aluko (Punch Newspaper), CSP. Monday Agbonika (Divisional Police Officer, Adeniji Adele Police Station), CSP. Olugbemi (Divisional Police Officer, Ilupeju Police Station), Mrs Chinwe Onyewku (Gender and Development Action).

This would be incomplete if I fail to acknowledge subsequent members of DSVRT, Ms Mosunmola Balogun (Directorate of Public Prosecutions), Mrs Fagbayi (Directorate of Public Prosecutions), Mrs Modupeola Sahid Adebambo, (Ministry of Youth and Social Development), Dr Okaga (Ministry of Health), Dr Victoria Omoera (Ministry of Health), Mrs Adeola Birch (Ministry of Health), Dr Veronica Iwayemi (Primary Health Care Board), Dr Oreolwa Finnih (Primary Health Care Board), Mr Akinremi (Family Social Services), Mrs Toyin Jaiyeola (Ministry of Women Affairs & Poverty Alleviation), Mrs Abiola Osinfowokan (Child Protection Unit, Ministry of Youth and Social Development), Mrs Bukola Salami (Office of Public Defender), Mrs Yinka Adeyemi (Office of Public Defender), Dr Babajide Martins, (Office of Public Defender). Some are still serving; some have retired and some have been posted to occupy other positions in the State Government.

I would also use this opportunity to appreciate the countless volunteers that have passed through the Office of the Coordinator of DSVRT, the first volunteer group, Tolulope Shonowo, Joy Ikeh, Adetayo Oshinowo, and Adesola Osuntoki.

To the engine room, the DSVRT Crew; Mrs Kemi Bello, Mrs Tumininu Oni, Ms Bunmi Orekoya, Mr Jeffrey Ekenkwo, Ms Tope Oyedija, Mr Damilare Adewusi, Mr Henry Okafor, Ms Abiola Odesanya, Ms Faith Olokun, Ms Doyin Awosika, you all are the real MVPs. Thank you for your commitment and passion.

I also appreciate the several National Youth Service Corps, particularly, Uche Ani, Kanyinsola Fadairo, Victor Ochega, Onyinye Muo, Tomi Ibadin and Tobi Williams.

I also appreciate the Virtual Gender-Based Violence call handlers, too many to mention. Thank you for understanding the vision and playing your parts in ensuring its actualisation.

To the support staff, Mr Sule Bello, Mr Roland Ogamune, Mr Adewale Joseph and Mr Kenny, thank you for providing the necessary backup structure.

The professionals, Mrs Oyekanmi, Mrs. Ajisafe, Mrs Dehinde Samuel, Ms Tolu Damilola, thank you for being ever so accommodating along the way as we navigated new waters.

I have been privileged to work with several development partners, Madam Jaiyeola Abiose of United Nations Population Fund (UNFPA), Ms Tosin Akhibu of United Nations (UN) Women, Dr Rabi of UNFPA, Mr Denise Onoise of UNICEF, Mrs Ajibola Ijimakinwa of RoLAC, Ms Olufunke Baruwa of Ford Foundation. Working with you all has been smooth and refreshing. Thank you for the partnership.

I also really appreciate the partners within the government over the years, especially Office of Education Quality Assurance, initially with Mrs Ronke Soyombo and then Mrs Abiola Seriki-Ayeni, officers from the Ministry of Youth and Social Development, particularly Mrs Odukoya and Mr Yakubu Jubril.

To the DSVRT's faculty of erudite facilitators and advisors, Prof. Ayodele Atsenuwa, Assoc. Prof. Olufunmilayo Bammeke, Mr Taiwo Akinlami, Mrs Lola Alonge, Dr Tolu Oko-Igaire, Dr Funmi Akinola, Mrs Olubola Akinsete, Dr. Jimi Sodipo and Ms Avril Edero, thank you for the support and particularly the friendship, through the years.

My appreciation goes to the various Non-Governmental Organisations, Civil Society Organisations, thank you for the cooperation and collaboration. Indeed, there is no telling what can be achieved when we work together.

I thank my in-laws, particularly the matriarch of the Adeniyi family, Mrs Ibironke Grace Adeniyi for loving me unconditionally.

To my darling husband and dearest friend, Oluwatobi Emmanuel Abiodun Adeniyi, thank you very much for your support. None of this could have been achieved without you. I also thank my children, Olatide Alexander Adeniyi, Araoluwa Nicole Adeniyi and Adedola Chigaemezu Adeniyi for being very supportive and understanding. Je t'aime tres forte.

To the thousands of survivors I am privileged to have met, I am broken because of your stories, but I'm the better for it.

10th January 2021.

FOREWORD

It is my pleasure to write the foreword for this book by 'Lola Vivour-Adeniyi, *LIVING FOR A HIGHER PURPOSE: inspiring hope through the Nigerian Public Service*. The book has chronicled the life and activities of Domestic and Sexual Violence Team under the Lagos State Ministry of Justice, from its inception in 2014 as a small unit under the then Attorney-General to a full-fledged agency with its own Executive Secretary. Written in easy to read language, it shows the struggles of a highly passionate lawyer, a civil servant, who battled with the often very bureaucratic public service system to set up a highly effective multi-sectorial coordinating organisation for sexual and domestic violence in Lagos State.

The book gives hope and guidance to every determined public servant who means to take steps to ensure the system functions maximally towards improving the lives of the ordinary citizen. Detail anecdotes of her interactions with her ministry and supervisor, important stakeholders in other ministries, the Nigerian Police Force, international development organisations like the UNFPA and the nongovernmental organisations, is a useful guide not only to young and upcoming public servants, but also to programme managers in development organisations who have to cope with the routine demands of constant innovations to solve problems and get things done under a structured and bureaucratic system.

'Lola has been described by those close to her as 'energetic and determined', a 'small woman who makes great things happen'. These have been aptly demonstrated in this book. Her focus, innovative thinking, ability to negotiate difficult proposals and eyes for what is right and just, stands her out as an asset for any organisation she works with. No doubt, her appointment as the first Executive Secretary of the DSVRT Agency is well deserved.

This book is recommended for every start-up programme officer and young civil servants determined to build their various careers and make their marks in the rapid developing world.

Ulla Elisabeth Mueller,
UNFPA Nigeria Resident Representative.

INTRODUCTION

The public service in Nigeria is not usually the first port of call for fresh graduates. From outside it looks dark and gloomy. That was my impression until my foray into the public sector in August, 2019.

Initially, I concede, I was very sceptical and suspicious of everyone and everything. That mood soon changed when I started reading submissions and write-ups by Lola. Realising that I had a gem in my hands, I quickly appointed her as one of my aides in September 2019. Lola's enthusiasm, passion, diligence, and sheer brilliance won me over and my impression about the public service gradually moved from dark and gloomy to one of profound luminescence.

The Lagos State Government is blessed to have Lola and several others like her in its workforce. By and large, Lola has been the engine room of the state's robust domestic and sexual violence response. All the accolades and encomiums showered on the state's response to the scourge that domestic and sexual violence has become, are linked to Lola's efforts.

I cannot count how many times Lola has infected me with her passion and nudged me—to sign one more letter or memo, start or attend one more campaign, make that extra phone call, push harder to get approvals and funds released. All these for the cause of protecting the vulnerable in our society. Her selflessness is inspiring and moving.

I trust that as she shares her odyssey through the public service in this debut, many people contemplating careers in the public service or even those on the verge of giving up on their careers in this sphere would use Lola's journey and success story as detailed in this book as a lightening-rod of some sort to chart their own path.

Moyosore Onigbanjo SAN FCIArb* is the 18th Attorney General and Commissioner for Justice, Lagos State.

DEDICATION

This book is dedicated to all survivors of Sexual and Gender Based Violence.

CHAPTER 1

IN THE BEGINNING

The door swung open to reveal Mr Ade Ipaye behind his desk, a brown obeche carved with precision; his sleeves rolled up on his arms, the black pen in his right hand working furiously on the A4 paper, his left hand cradled. The office resembled a white void save the black TV, the grey Macbook that lay open on the spacious brown office table, and other things of colours to distort the white infinity. It was July 2014, I was his Personal Assistant on legal matters. I entered with a national daily that headlined a case of a child that had been defiled. The publication contravened all child protection measures: the identity of the child, her address, details of her family members—everything was published in black and white.

I declared my concerns to my boss, Mr Ade Ipaye, and he suggested that we took up the defilement case. He instructed that I drafted a letter for his signature to the Deputy Commissioner of Police to request the duplicate case file so that he, through the Director of Public Prosecutions would pursue the case.

That month alone, we had prepared over five letters requesting the police to forward the duplicate case file. It was not the first time we have had to do that, and as usual, we had to face lots of hurdles as the police weren't forthcoming and swift to act on our demands. My morale dampened into gloom like rainclouds gathering; my countenance sank like the axe head of the prophets into the waters. All I was left with were a bunch of endless letters like a bouquet of withering roses, yet a pulse of hope thumped in my heart. My boss noticed my crestfallenness and asked that we sought other legal ways of combatting Domestic and Sexual Violence within appropriate jurisdictions.

After some days, I returned with more letters that needed to be signed and dispatched. As soon as I finished dispatching the letters, I began researching into what was obtainable in other jurisdictions. I checked what was applicable both nationally and internationally; how jurisdictions like England, Scandinavia States, and the United States of America are able to provide swift response to Sexual and Gender Based Violence. In the process of researching, lots of questions breezed in and out of my mind—some carrying with them answers that bloomed while some fell on rocky grounds and expired. I found myself asking questions like: what are the indicators and indices of sexual violence? What measures have been taken by other societies to tackle cases of sexual violence?

As these questions reverberated in my head, forming a trail for which I must follow, as if to say: this is where all questions get their answers, I discovered most civilised states had policies and laws that were duly enforced while also providing medical services and institutions that offered holistic support to both victims and survivors of sexual violence.

I was made to understand, through my research, that the government was the key provider of core services; states collaborated with Civil Society organisations to ensure adequate care for survivors were provided. In instances where this was not being done, Civil Society Organisations would rise to the challenge and call out Government institutions to do what was required of them.

The research opened me to several cases of Gender- Based Violence and how they were being tackled; I was surprised to learn that intervention services had to be survivor-centred—everything the government did to salvage such situations revolved around the survivor. This knowledge nestled in my soul, and I carried it with me like a prayer through this grassy path. 'This is not about me, or my colleagues, but rather, about the survivors that we are looking to assist,' I often told myself when faced with any case of sexual violence.

I must confess, happening upon this knowledge shaped my perspective on the issues as well as influenced the various interventions I have been able to propose and implement.

Finally, after one week of dispatching letters and watching as hope flickered, happiness anchored on our shores. The concept of the Lagos State Domestic and Sexual Violence Response Team was curated. Contrary to what was generally obtainable, either Sexual Assault Referral Team which focused on only Sexual Violence, or a Domestic Violence agency which focused solely on Domestic Violence and Intimate Partner Violence. It was proposed that for Lagos, it should be both Domestic and Sexual Violence. The thinking was that we use one approach to address the menace that manifests in different forms.

This news reached our office with glee, and the excitement loomed over our heads. The flickering hope steadied, bright like fluorescence. I was asked to develop the concept note by Mr Ipaye. My conversation with him was refreshing; 'we are going to make a headway in this case' he said, expanding his lips into a smile. He gave approval to proceed and asked that I worked with Mr Akingbolahan Adeniran, a senior colleague, especially as we had an assignment which was to assemble the team.

CHAPTER 2

ASSEMBLING THE TEAM

The assemblage of the team began the next day when I arrived at the office. Everyone beamed with ecstasy. Optimism smeared the faces of my colleagues, entangled with the frigid air wafting from the air conditioner that stood like a mannequin at a corner. I and few of my colleagues who would later become my team members embarked on a study to ascertain the key responder agencies at that time. We considered the broad areas of focus and categorised them as follows: Medical &Psychosocial, Legal, Law enforcement, Social services and other support services—after which we based the success of the team on the provision of legal, psychological, emergency and rescue, law enforcement, empowerment and Alternative Dispute Resolution services.

The task of assembling a team was a herculean one. My brains laboured themselves in contemplation. On my desk, heaps of papers stranded themselves. Around me were potential teammates, who were also my colleagues, bracing themselves for the job that was soon going to be before them. This led me to the knowledge that most of them already have their jobs, so I had to provide alternatives in which we could carry out the work effectively like leveraging on technologies.

The composition was critical. Knowing this, I primed myself to give a speech, to motivate them, to lead them out of the clutches of self-doubt and into hope, faith and effort. As the frigid air continued wafting from the air conditioner making my hands as cold as a dog's nose, I stood up, tugged at my clothes as if to arrange them properly and said to my team members, 'working in this space requires passion, commitment, competence, care and skill. But passion, in my humble opinion, comes first. We therefore need passionate officers and individuals already working in this space to serve as members of the team'.

My speech was brief. Perhaps, my anxiety caused it; however, was enough to inspire them. But I was buoyed when one of us stood up and said,

'Yes, it is true and I pledge to be passionate about the work we are going to do here.'

While still assembling the team, I took into consideration that support services were provided for by both government and non-governmental organisations: therefore, it was a necessity for us to have representation from both sectors.

Similarly, though championed by the Attorney-General's office, the DSVRT was not a legal entity. Rather, it envisaged an unprecedented level of collaboration amongst responder agencies. (I would eventually find out in the future that this was going to be problematic).

We would need top level representatives from the different agencies, who would be nominated either by their parent ministries or their organisations to serve. These members should be able to take decisions, and should not be on a rotational basis, lest it becomes the stereotypical agency 'committee/task force' where people are sent to represent a member. (This was particularly applicable to the public servants).

All these problematic indexes posed as a great inhibitor, and I wrote various letters to various ministries towards reparation. Ministries like: the Ministry of Health, Ministry of Women Affairs & Poverty Alleviation, Office of Youth, Sports and Social Development, Ministry of Education, Office of Public Defender and the Directorate of Public Relations.

The letters sent to the various Commissioners were crystal and emphatic; we wanted key members of their teams and required active participation. We also needed nominees to be able to take decisions, hence the insistence on top level representations. If this was supposed to work, we couldn't operate within the limits of red tape and bureaucracy that ultimately had the potential of killing the initiative before it even began.

The selection process for NGOs was critical and painstaking. However, Lagos State is blessed to host NGOs doing amazing works in the communities. One of such NGOs is Partnership for Justice. A year before the establishment of DSVRT, Partnership for Justice had created and launched the Mirabel Centre, the first Sexual Assault Referral Centre in Nigeria. We had been intimated about their services, and it was felt that they would be indispensable to the Team. Lagos State Gender Advocacy Team, Gender and Development Action (GADA) and State Accountability Voice Initiative were also nominated. We had to identify an NGO that had strong community presence, and our research led us to Women's Rights and Health Project which had for the past two decades, done community development work in the largest Local Government Area in Nigeria, Alimosho.

The selection of the police was also critical. At that time, Justice for All had recently established Model Police Stations in three divisions, Isokoko, Adeniji Adele and Ilupeju Police Stations. Officers in these specialised police stations, also referred to as Family Support Units, had been trained on best practices for investigating and prosecuting cases of Sexual and Gender Based Violence. Their formations were also designed; the composition of the unit was very strategic, at least 98% of staff strength were women. At that time, I had not yet visited any of the Family Support Units, but this is wat I was told.

There was, however, an incident that was remarkable in helping us select police officers. On a fateful day in a fateful month in 2014 when the sun clutched itself to the infinite sky, I accompanied my boss to a function on Sexual and Gender- Based Violence. On our way there, from the windscreen of the car, I saw hawkers litter the road with their wares. Men, women, but mostly out-of-school children. This sight lingered in my head until we arrived at the venue—I kept asking myself, 'don't they have parents?' 'Do their parents know how prone they are to being sexually abused?'

Arriving at the venue, we were given the programme of event. I checked through it and saw that the Deputy Governor of Lagos State, Her Excellency, Princess Orelope-Adefulire, who was also superintending the Ministry of Women Affairs and Poverty Alleviation was going to be present at the event as the Special Guest of Honour.

After Her Excellency spoke, a police officer was invited to make some remarks. He introduced himself as SP Monday Agbonika, and as he spoke, I marvelled at his oration. I would have doubted he was a law enforcement officer if he was not in uniform (kudos to the Nigerian Police who despite the often-negative rap they have, are still able to churn out extremely professional and capable officers). He spoke with great precision. I could feel his voice slither out of his mouth with prolificity. He talked about the lapses in the system, the plight of survivors, the need for institutions to be strengthened; he talked about what was possible with the police force if adequate resources were made available. He touched on stigma, and the role of society in ensuring we increase victims' safety and offenders' responsibility.

Granted, this was not the first time I had met him. Once, on 17 May 2014, I was asked to represent my boss at the launching of the Adeniji Adele Family Support Unit. The event was filled with bodies like a pebble drowned in water, was swallowed up by the multitude of people that wanted to exchange pleasantries with him. Though I did not get the opportunity to have a conversation with him, SP Monday Agbonika was a breath of fresh air, and he had to be on the Team! I certainly had to meet him after the event.

Meeting him was a big deal because I was an introvert some sort, but his words were too compelling to let this opportunity slide. After a long thought, I summoned up the last courage left in my blood, walked through the afternoon crowd that clustered here and there to introduce myself to him.

'Hello Sir, my name is Titilola Vivour-Adeniyi,' I said, expanding my orifice into a grin.

'Hello Ma, I guess you already know me; however, I am SP Monday Agbonika, and I work for the Nigerian Police Force' he replied.

I saw questions sprawl over his face. He must have been wondering what business I had, coming to introduce myself to him. But due to his line of work, he had to keep his calm and entertain me, regardless. I informed him of our intention and how he had to be on the Team. He needed no convincing, he also echoed the need for the other Divisional Police Officers of the other- two Family Support Units to be informed and nominated to serve as members.

We had finally gotten our composition[1]- representatives from: Attorney-General & Commissioner for Justice, The Police Force (Family Support Units), Sexual Assault Referral Centre- MIRABEL, Office of the Public Defender, Directorate of Citizens' Rights, Directorate of Public Prosecutions, Ministry of Health, Ministry of Women Affairs & Poverty Alleviation, Ministry of Education, Office of Youth and Social Development (OYSD), NGOs (WRAHP, LASGAT, SAVI), Media (Channels TV and Punch Newspaper).

It was agreed that there should be a Chairman, naturally, and since the Ministry of Justice was championing the cause, the Hon. Attorney General served as the Chairman. Nevertheless, we needed someone to coordinate the response machinery, the activities of the team and to ensure we carried out our objectives. I was requested to serve as Coordinator.

It was 9 September 2014. We had invited members of the 4th realm to provide press coverage for the inauguration of the team. I remember at the inaugural meeting; I was seated to the left of the Attorney General. The hall brimmed with people, names I only read in newspapers. I tottered out lastly to introduce myself and Mr Ipaye was beside himself with laughter.

'Coordinator,' he called me. 'She is the coordinator of the team,' he said to the rest of the people. 'Better get used to that designation,' he nosed at me.

We laughed into the birth of the magic. I am not sure if at that moment, we knew what we had signed up for, or the extent of the influence we would have, both individually and collectively. However, passion and doggedness kept us, glued us together. Like pillars, it kept us standing despite the weight of work ahead.

---

[1] The composition has since been expanded

CHAPTER 3

RUNNING AN OFFICE WITH NO BUDGET

What I have come to understand about governments is that most initiatives without directives are commenced without any budgetary allocation. Running the DSVRT office was not an exception. We operated the office for a whole year without a budget. I had no one to support or assist me. Bearing in mind that no Office of Coordinator had been created, there was no running cost, nor financial support. This was also during the period where Governor Babatunde Raji Fashola's administration was winding up, and we were heading into an intense political season (late 2014/early 2015).

This period was my baptism into the concept of volunteerism because it got to a stage, approximately four months after the Team was inaugurated that it became clear that I obviously could not do this on my own. Interestingly, we did not put out any advertisement or notice for volunteers. It was therefore a blessing when the first volunteer, Tolulope George reached out, and indicated her willingness to volunteer pending when she would be able to perform her compulsory National Youth Service Corps (NYSC) program. Since then, we have had over 45 volunteers serve in various capacities, some of them without receiving any financial remuneration for their efforts.

When I look back, I realise that the months of June – December 2015 were some of the busiest months for me. Shortly after H.E., Mr Babatunde Raji Fashola, SAN left the office and my boss had gone to Abuja to resume his new position as Deputy Chief of Staff to Mr President, there wasn't much certainty as to what my fate or the team's fate would be. Mine was even more precarious, bearing in mind that I was not a civil servant. What would become of me? Would I still be privileged to serve as an assistant to the incoming Attorney-General? What would happen to DSVRT? We had no legislative enactment binding us. What would become of us? These questions weighed me down like a tonne of bricks tied to the back of a drowning person; still, I paddled the currents because I had to be strong for myself and the team.

Apart from being pregnant, this was a defining moment as His Excellency, Mr Akinwunmi Ambode had just assumed office. As is customary with every administration, one is not sure of the agenda of the incumbent, since it only unfolds with his unfolding days in office. With the uncertainty, the focus was the task at hand.

Running DSVRT was my sole endeavour at the time. I had ceased being a Personal Assistant to the Hon. Attorney General. I took a pay cut. My monthly salary, previously at ₦130,000 was now ₦30,000, an amount I would receive for the next 4 years as a 'Project Officer'. Esteemed members of the DSVRT had primary jobs; their involvement in the DSVRT was on an ad hoc basis, and if the team was to dissolve, they still had their offices and organisations they would continue to work with. Everyone would move on with their lives. And so, necessity was on me to make effective and successful the initiative until it was institutionalised. Therefore, passion and reason joined forces to spur us on. We were going to make a lot of noise about our cause since we had no funds. So much noise that we wouldn't be ignored. It worked.

On a fateful day in the ember months of 2015, Mr Makinde, an officer in Planning Department, Ministry of Justice, approached me and asked if I was not going to submit a budget for my 'office'. He spoke, 'Is this not an office? Don't you need running cost? Lola, write a proposal and request a budget in 2016'.

With guidance from appropriate factions, our budget was prepared and submitted. At that time, I didn't think much of it. I refused to give in to the thought that we would have a budget in the coming year, because I did not want my hopes to be dashed. I believed that if we were purposefully busy, one way or the other, we would get funding.

I was ecstatic when I saw the Domestic Violence Code make it into the budget, and the amount approved for it. Indeed, our work had begun speaking for us and we were being noticed even at the very top. Sometime in mid-2016, I received a call from the then Solicitor-General and Permanent Secretary, Ms Funlola Odunlami. She said Governor Akinwunmi Ambode had been impressed with our work and wanted to know what we needed as a team. She asked that I work with the Director of Citizen's Rights, the amiable Mrs Omotilewa Ibirogba to put some details on paper.

We came up with a memorandum stating the different projects we wanted to undertake—various activities geared towards strengthening the capacity of responder agencies to adequately respond to incidents of Sexual and Gender-Based Violence. At the same time, empowering residents of Lagos with vital information on support services through outdoor advertising, radio jingles, social media advocacy, the whole works.

We included the need for more shelter homes, and we requested the transformation of DSVRT into a fully functioning structured unit that manages the day to day activities of DSVRT. This would ensure a streamlined single point of contact as regards the management of databases, liaising with Government and private enterprises as well as other numerous daily and weekly deliverables that require detailed focus.

We required office space for five core staff of the team which comprised the Coordinator, two support staff and two volunteers/interns including the remuneration of the officers (including myself). Every item was approved except the last one because he wanted to observe our operations before committing to this. It was still perfectly fine. At last, we had funds to embark on some innovations which were critical in laying the foundation for our response mechanism in the state. I am often asked how I did it. How without funding I was able to organise programmes, conduct trainings and ensured the media publicised our various activities?

My counterparts in other states reached out when their response teams got inaugurated, and they asked the same set of questions—sometimes my response is always the same— passion, commitment, tenacity and resilience. It is a calling that fuels me to keep going, even when it seems like I've hit a brick wall. Also, leveraging on relationships, partnerships, and people in your networks to provide services gratis and ultimately, having the right support from the people you work with, including your peers and line management will take you a long way. I was fortunate over the years to work with directors, permanent secretaries, and of course attorneys general, who were committed to this cause.

CHAPTER 4

ACCESSING DONOR FUNDING/ SUPPORT AND NOT LETTING A CRISIS (COVID-19) GO TO WASTE

When we started operations in 2014, I identified donors, development partners, working in this space, studied their portfolios and then developed proposals and concept notes tailored towards their respective mandates.

Unfortunately, we did not receive any response for the first letters we sent out. At that time, I had not built a rapport or relationship with the individual donors. Whenever we would see at functions, and I introduce myself, some would say, 'oh, Mrs Adeniyi, I've heard about you, keep up the good work at DSVRT,' and that would be all.

One of those days, I had the opportunity to attend a function and most of the donors were represented. The venue of the event was filled with people whom I felt could be our donors, but were not. I joked to the lady seated next to me, wearing an expensive gown draped in glittering stones, 'Is it that you do not think we are working?' 'Of course, we know you people are working, the issue is that donor funding is given to line ministries, and DSVRT is not a line ministry,' she replied with all the politeness she could muster.

According to her, her organisation was experiencing some challenges in fixing us in a box as we were involved in cross-cutting sectors of health, legal, security, enforcement, advocacy, etc. There was no *line ministry* regulating all these sectors. Also, as a team, we did not have a law establishing its operation so we were a bit handicapped in that regard.

This however did not deter me in my quest for accessing funds. We received more visibility as we proceeded, and were able to invite the donors to attend our programmes.

Asides requesting financial support, we also indicated our willingness to receive technical support. UNAIDS and UNFPA were very willing to provide technical support towards the actualisation of the upgrade of Primary Health Care Centres. Dr Asa from UNAIDS as well as the Late Mrs Damilola Obinna from UNFPA reviewed the draft, Sexual Assault Standing Order, and made their input. Late Mrs Damilola Obinna served as a facilitator when we commenced thc trainings for doctors.

We found out that some donors would not give funds directly, but they would provide everything you require for your programme; venue, catering, resource materials, transportation allowance for attendees, facilitators' fees etc. The Rule of Law and Anti-Corruption (RoLAC), under the British Council was one of such donors. We worked with Mrs Ajibola Ijimakinwa in organising trainings for the police as well as religious clerics and judicial officers. We were also able to organise round table discussions in partnership with nongovernmental organisations.

When COVID-19 struck, most of the team's services had to be taken virtually. I remember, during that period, various organisations, including donor agencies began to leverage on applications, including Zoom to organise meetings. It was also an opportunity to share experiences, identify challenges and proffer solutions.

One of such occasions, I joined the zoom call organised by a donor agency, and I was asked to share experience on our response to SGBV during COVID-19. It was not easy as much as it was not totally a difficult task since we were keeping data of the number of cases being handled and the number of mediations we had provided virtually. I said to myself 'this is the time to bare yourself; to peel your plight into the eyes of those that can help you'. So, after reeling out the statistics, I used the opportunity to quickly highlight some of the challenges we were experiencing which included a lack of airtime and internet (data).

We also required stipends for drivers and officers who would have to risk their lives to embark on rescue missions during the complete restriction of movement.

As soon as I finished speaking, a lady whom I learnt is Dr Rabiatu Sageer, replied, 'My organisation, UNFPA will be willing to support you with what you need for at least a month.'

A little silence ensued. I could see the surprise printed like letters on the faces of my colleagues. I made to thank her but she continued, 'this would be done through The Women's Helping Hands Initiative (TWHI).'

I later learned that TWHI is an implementing partner non-governmental organisation, founded by H.E. Mrs Dolapo Osinbajo. And this would mark the beginning of our relationship with UNFPA.

During the one-month period, we received funds, and we provided the report of the various activities we had embarked on. A month after this, I received a phone call from TWHI to join a meeting with UNFPA to further deliberate our procedures for response during the pandemic. This was of utmost importance in view that despite the slight relaxation of movement, survivors were still experiencing difficulties in accessing the office. The opportunity for a call centre presented itself. At that time, we had just secured our toll-free line (08000333333), so I informed UNFPA of this and suggested the call centre idea. This, I felt, was of utmost importance, especially in view of the directives from the State Government to maintain a skeletal workforce. Most of my staff were not coming into the office, so attending to clients in the office was almost not an option at that time.

Indeed, COVID-19 and the subsequent restriction of movements emphasised the need for us to fully embrace and leverage on technology in delivering our services. During or post COVID-19, one thing remained sacrosanct, survivors must continue to have access to support services.

During the virtual meetings, Dr Rabi and her team suggested the need to have a Gender Based Violence Virtual Referral and Response Service. This would basically enable survivors, mandated reporters, and other vulnerable groups have easy access and links to all sectors responding to Domestic and Sexual Violence cases.

The dream was to ensure callers would be able to access the following services: Health Clinical Management of Rape (CMR); Social Services—Psychosocial Support (PSS); and Protection—Security and Access to justice. These services would be delivered at no cost to clients whilst maintaining the principles of Survivor Centred Approach, Safety and Confidentiality. Leveraging on the toll-free line that was recently secured, we would need to design an application or a software that would enable us to receive calls, make escalations, refer to other responder agencies, etc.

These were the seasons of new realities, the pandemic shifted perspectives to new landscapes and occasioned mutations of pedestal and mundane activities to technological postures like never before. The paradigm shift, at the time, was inevitable as a new culture was imminent.

Incidentally, around that same time, I had received an email from Mteja, a subsidiary of Africa's Talking. They indicated their interest in setting up a call centre for DSVRT which would operate around the clock every day of the week. It would however be accessible remotely. I had a meeting with Mr Ndubuisi Agbeyeke, Precious Ejiro and Stephany to learn about the operations of the technology.

The only concern was that we would not own the software, and this raised various data privacy concerns for us. I had imagined the threat of confidentiality that we might face as it is our duty to maintain all survivors' privacy—I cannot say exactly how, but I felt the weight of guilt on me as if I had already divulged all survivors' information. This was the kind of burden that accompanied the work, especially when done with utmost passion. This concern was however addressed by the development of the team's own application. Going forward, an opportunity presented itself, so I introduced Mteja to UNFPA, and that was the beginning of a great and fruitful partnership. Aside from the technology that would have to be built, we would also require hardware; laptops, mobile phones, uninterrupted internet (data) supply and trained personnel who would also need to be engaged to operate the telephone lines.

Besides being trained, these personnel had to be empathetic and possess relevant leadership with communication and interpersonal relationship skills to calm situations, as well as be knowledgeable about the way the DSVRT operated. The personnel had to be able to inspire hope in the hearts of the callers whilst acting with a sense of urgency. The round the-clock operation of the centre every day, all week would require the officers to work a shift.

Fortunately for us, in time past, we had embarked on various research and community engagements and our foot soldiers were students drawn from the Faculty of Social Sciences in University of Lagos. We therefore believed it was a perfect fit to consider these professionals for the role of GBV call handler. The recruitment process was done jointly by my office and UNFPA. At the end of the exercise, fourteen social workers were selected and trained for the position.

It was not an easy task. My team and I went through the hurdles of setting up a training space and availing the necessary equipment for the training of personnel. At a point, I felt the sun bite into my flesh; I felt it trapped between pebbles of sweat and the pores from which they stoked. Running around was not easy, not for me and definitely not for my team. But I thought to myself, is this not what passion is? To hold both rose and thorns; to work tirelessly for the survival of the organisation and the survivors.

The project also identified the need to provide certain services virtually, including telemedicine, legal support/ advice, psychological first aid as well as emergency support. We identified and recruited professionals in these fields for this purpose. Gratefully, while we already had clinical psychologists working with us, we however had to engage other clinicians and lawyers from the International Federation of Women Lawyers (FIDA) to assist in this regard.

Money is a great booster of morale. A reward for work, an expression of gratitude and motivation for more. We agreed to place key responder agencies on monthly stipends to encourage them. More so, Officers in Charge of Family Support Units, the health sector, and social welfare.

We deliberated the locale of the call centre—the convenience of working remotely due to COVID-19 restrictions against the confidentiality and professional conduct of officers.

In the thick of deliberations, we discovered that we could be assigned a space in the Lagos State Command Control Centre, operated by the Lagos State Emergency Management Agency (LASEMA). To that effect, we drafted to the Ministry of Special Duties as well as the General Manager of LASEMA, Dr Olufemi Oke-Osanyintolu, and our proposition was approved. Situated with all other emergency responders including the Rapid Response Squad (RRS) of the Lagos State Police Command, Lagos

State Traffic Management Authority (LASTMA), Fire Service and Lagos State Ambulance Service (LASAMBUS), it meant that we would be able to leverage on the emergency response apparatus of the State.

It was a perfect affair. Officers would be in a secure location—which was of paramount concern to us—especially for the night shift. There was unlimited access to internet services and state-of-the-art facilities. This was also an opportunity to begin to integrate response to Sexual and Gender-Based Violence into the State's emergency response machinery.

On 1 January 2021, we commenced operations and the feedback was encouraging. In the first nine months of operation, the GBV VRRS received over 15,481 calls, out of which 1323 were actual cases of domestic and sexual violence.

Around the same time, we started engaging with UNFPA in March 2020, Mr Dabesaki from Ford Foundation reached out to us. This was an exciting experience because in time past, I had written to Ford Foundation, introducing and re-introducing DSVRT, showcasing our different activities and highlighting areas we hoped would be mutually beneficial, unfortunately, no response came forth.

That day was like every other day, I had stepped into the office hoping to do some paper work, send out letters to likeminded organisations for assistance and attend to survivors.

However, an hour into the work, I received a call, a call that would change my mood for the rest of the day. The voice on the other end of the call was mild and polite.

'Am I on to Titilola, the head of DSVRT?' he asked.

'Yes, you are,' I replied.

'I am Dabesaki from Ford foundation and I am calling to let you know that we are pleased with the work going on in DSVRT, and would like to collaborate with the Response Team,' he stated.

I was overwhelmed, I held the phone for a second, speechless, as though my words got stuck in my throat on their way out. It was no hidden thing that an opportunity to receive support had presented itself and DSVRT was identified and considered to benefit from this grant. We were asked what our priority areas of focus were and we identified the need to strengthen our coordination processes.

Law enforcement and the provision of medical services were of utmost concern for us. We believed it had become necessary to upgrade at least five additional Divisions of the Lagos State Police Command to the status of Family Support Unit.

Also, we identified the need to select pilot private hospitals that would be willing to provide sexual assault management services to survivors. Again, we identified the need for survivors of domestic and sexual violence to receive psycho social support at the Primary Health Centres. These were efforts towards survivors' holistic care and support.

A concept note was developed to highlight the gaps we sought to fill and how this would affect our ability to deliver our core mandate which was to coordinate response.

Gratefully, this was approved by Ford management and we were able to commence activities. Over one hundred and fifty nurses from all the Comprehensive Primary Health Centres and General Hospitals were trained on the provision of psycho-social support.

We were also able to upgrade Okokomaiko, Epe, Bariga, Owutu (Ikorodu) as well as Ajegunle Police Divisions. These divisions were selected scientifically, leveraging on data of reported cases from those local government areas as well as community engagements in those areas.

Finally, we were able to identify five pilot private hospitals already empanelled on the Lagos State Health Insurance Scheme under the aegis of Lagos State Health Management Agency (LASHMA). These pilot private health facilities located across the metropolis were also provided with Rape Kits as well as data reporting tools to standardise reporting in the State. These private hospitals include R-Jolad, Bee Hess, New Merit, Faleti Medical Centre and Mobonike Hospital & Maternity Home.

Our agenda was an encompassing one. It made people wonder why we didn't limit provision of medical support to only government hospitals and the Sexual Assault Referral Centres because here we were extending a hand of fellowship to private hospitals. But our quest to make services easily accessible to survivors was at the forefront of our objectives. If a survivor was more comfortable approaching a private hospital to access immediate medical attention after a traumatic experience, then we should ensure that option was available.

As much as the need to make medical support accessible through private hospitals could be regarded as a more logical decision, to be honest, it first came from an innate sense of empathy for survivors. I thought of the encumbrance survivors would have to go through standing on a long queue at one of the government hospitals, waiting to be attended to. I thought of the many number of bodies shuffling in and out of such hospitals, I thought of the discomfort it would bring to some people, so I thought of engaging private hospitals.

In addition to my many thoughts, COVID-19 reinforced the fact that we could not afford to have monopoly of provision of services. In terms of policy formulation, as a team, we were fortunate to receive donor support from UN Women. This support was with a view to developing the

Lagos State Unified Response Protocol and Referral Pathway, which would outline a state-wide, unified, consistent response to cases of Domestic and Sexual Violence from survivor support service providers, law enforcement, prosecutors, and the courts. This, we believed would foster and strengthen synergy between and within Responder Agencies. We thought this was very compelling as the absence of a unified document was one of the lacunas that was identified when representatives of the various UN offices visited the Team in November 2019.

With a unified response protocol document, we would be able to effectively discharge the primary duty of ensuring effective coordination of services across all relevant responder agencies. The document was developed and reviewed jointly by representatives of the responder agencies and in order to ensure acceptability and implementation, it was decided that the policy makers would append their signature in the endorsement portion. The Hon. Commissioners for Health, Education, and Women Affairs & Poverty Alleviation and of course the Hon. Attorney General and Commissioner for Justice. The Hon. Chief Judge as well as a representative of the non-governmental organisation also endorsed the policy document.

This brought me more joy. Who could have imagined that a movement that began with the need to rescue one girl, to set one story right would turn into a fully-grown organisation with supports from influential people? To tell the truth, if one were to peek inside of my heart, one would see a flutter of butterflies. I cannot explain the happiness that I felt, except that it reached my bones, soothing like a balm. I do not know if the reason for my happiness hinged on the fact that I had the commissioner of Women Affairs & Poverty Alleviation and other notable persons append their signatures to the document or that we were making tremendous progress, but I do know that I was full of joy.

Part of the project summary included the need to train service providers on the usability of the policy document. Consequently, we trained the first three hundred officers and personnel comprising government, non-governmental organisations, the Police, the academia, the judiciary, customary court judges, the media, traditional rulers, community leaders as well as religious leaders.

Asides from the policy document which was developed and the subsequent trainings, it was important to take into cognisance that Data collection on GBV was hampered by a lack of a central GBV data collection mechanism.

Indeed, the COVID-19 pandemic had posed a new challenge for responders of SGBV cases, as it became glaring that in order to preserve data and records of SGBV reports being made, a central data collection and reporting platform was needed. This would afford responders the opportunity to respond virtually, ruling out the limitations faced by providing responses to SGBV cases physically.

We therefore included the need to develop a Domestic and Sexual Violence Case Management System, (DSVCMS). As the name implied, the DSVCMS would be a Case Information/Data Management System, that synchronised Domestic and Sexual Violence Information inputted from the various accredited responder agencies.

I have always found it unethical and unprofessional for sensitive cases to be reported via social media platforms like WhatsApp, especially when such cases are shared on my private phone. Some cases may fall through the cracks, and there would not be an opportunity to automatically identify such cases and ascertain their statuses.

Fortunately, UN Women understood and appreciated the need to continuously leverage on technology and proceeded to approve the development of the case management application as one of the components in the project.

The DSVCMS as at the time this book was being written had been developed and was being used in the office and was about to be deployed to all relevant responder agencies for usage.

Working with donor agencies is beneficial because they are able to provide both technical and financial support. Granted, I have heard from colleagues who have had difficult experiences with donor agencies, especially trying to access support. Complaints such as bureaucracy, slow response and stringent conditions applied to the grants can be a discouraging factor.

Nonetheless, I have been privileged to work with amazing donor agencies and personnel. Personnel who understand what the issues are, and not simply interested in ticking boxes. Personnel who are results oriented, flexible and genuinely interested in the success of whatever initiative is sought to be implemented.

My experience with working with donors is that you need visibility; they need to know what you are doing and what you are doing should be related to their mandate.

Indeed, there is an art for writing successful proposals. But ultimately, it is important that once you *break in* to the 'world of donors' you maintain and sustain that relationship, especially leveraging on data to buttress your position and projects. Unfortunately, I learned all these in the most difficult of ways as I seldom had knowledge of how the donor world operated and how I could access it.

CHAPTER 5

SYSTEMATIC INSTITUTIONAL CHALLENGES

After the team was inaugurated, we lacked the funds to embark on trainings. I do not know exactly what was in the mind of my team members but for me, the passion was just blossoming, and needed faith as water, to bloom to fruition, and I let that happen. We prepared a five-year plan for ourselves and tried to identify the issues plaguing the different response sectors.

For the police, at that time, we had three Family Support Units, model police stations, established by the Justice 4 All Department for Innovation Initiative. This was such a great initiative as it sought to lessen the trauma survivors may experience upon contact with law enforcement. It was also critical in ensuring that only competently skilled police officers responded to cases. This could not be overemphasised as research has shown that the Police is usually a first responder, so the way police officers respond to survivors who are desirous of reporting cases would go a long way in determining whether or not the survivor would still be interested in pursuing justice. Accordingly, I particularly embraced this initiative.

However, we knew that three divisions were not sufficient to serve the entire metropolis, so we began to study the operation of the Family Support Unit and how we could scale up this amazing initiative.

I worked closely with SP Monday Agbonika. Regardless of where he was posted, he found a way of establishing a Family Support Unit in his Division/Command.

Still, we encountered certain difficulties, an example is the frequency of transfers of police officers—a testament that the road was not going to be rosy and even if it was, there were going to be thorns all over the stem. Police officers could be posted at any time, posted out of State or posted to other formations. And so, while we were eager to build capacity, we were also worried that we did not have control over how long the officers would remain in the particular Division. A lot of resources were deployed towards this cause, including human and financial. Imagine how heart breaking it can be when you begin to build relationships and suddenly, you are informed that the officer has been transferred to Kebbi State.

As such, we knew that the Police formation was not entirely under our control, but something had to be done to ensure we institutionalise our training curriculum on best practices for investigating and prosecuting Sexual and Gender Based Violence so that irrespective of the station an officer is posted, they are taught at the Police Training School. This looked like the most realistic solution to this issue pending when the proposition for state police would be favourably considered.

Getting it right at the investigation stage is primary, as cases are won at investigation stage not in court. The ability to conduct investigations that corroborate the disclosures of the survivor or exonerate suspects was and remain a key priority in responding to Sexual and Gender-Based Violence. Police officers had to move from desk investigation to visiting the scene of the crime, speaking to witnesses, placing the survivor at the scene, and ensuring statements of the survivors were properly recorded.

At that time, the police were heavily reliant on the use of confessional statements made by the suspects. However, the legal considerations had not been adhered to, sometimes due to lack of resources or ignorance of the law. This was negatively affecting the prosecution in court as most defendants would later reject the confessional statement, citing duress and then there would be a trial within the trial which would drag the case longer than necessary. If the court believed that the defendant confessed without duress, the evidence would be admissible.

It was however clear that this was no longer sustainable. Science had evolved and now, medical examination of survivors after sexual assault could be detailed enough to guide the police as well as aid the prosecution.

Investigating and prosecuting the offence of Rape was very technical. Successful convictions were few and far between. This alleged offence involved two adults; how is there proving that there was no consent? In the absence of a witness, in the absence of evidence of a struggle or violence, it most times became a case of 'he did it; I did not do it'.

We also had feedback from what certain police officers would say to the survivors, 'you too, is this what you wore?'; 'did he force you to come to his house?'; 'after he took you out for shopping and lunch, what were you expecting?'; 'madam, he said you are his girlfriend'; 'he said you people have been sleeping together, that this is not the first time'.

These sorts of responses are not limited to police officers by the way; it is a reflection of how our society views some of these issues. And most of the time, I am heartbroken when I hear cases of such responses.

These were enough to shatter a survivor's hope of getting justice. The institution that is to assist, does not believe a survivor's story, and so she leaves, worse off than she was before going to the police. She begins to blame herself again, she breaks into pieces, running away from the vestiges of her past; from the haunting claws of memories, to the testimony of the police, to learned helplessness, drenched in doubt, and contemplating, 'perhaps, I am to blame'. Then, silence—a silence that emboldens the suspect to perpetrate more of such crimes. But it does not end as a single story. Loud laughter and ridicule are the greetings of a man reporting domestic abuse.

It is a similar experience for an adolescent survivor. Reprimand without pity, mockery sans empathy. Certain police officers taunt them instead about their being biologically developed. I remember a case when the police officer could not conceal her bias towards the 16-year-old girl, simply because she was, in the police officer's words, '*well endowed*' and '*her eye has opened'*.

Certain police officers would encourage the suspect to beg the child's family, and sometimes even facilitate an out of court settlement. It was even more tragic if the adolescent had become pregnant because of the sexual abuse. Considerations like, 'if we jail the man, who will take care of the child?'; 'it has already been done, maybe he can marry her' were deciding factors for determining if the case was charged to court or not. These scenarios may sound like quotes culled from the scripts of a movie. However, this was the reality, it was happening, and unfortunately, it is still happening.

Despite the foregoing, we recorded some modest successes with cases of defilement. Turns out, children are generally believable. Of course, a 3-year-old girl cannot give consent. Most police officers would be enthusiastic about *getting justice* for the child. We, however still experienced some challenges in recording witness statements. Contrary to best practices, the statements were not being recorded in the words of the child, consequently, a good defence counsel would not hesitate to puncture holes in the case.

It was therefore of utmost importance that the police were properly trained on best practices for investigating Sexual and Gender-Based Violence cases. A manual had to be developed for this purpose, officers also had to have copies of the relevant laws, and they had to be empowered to appropriately make timely and necessary referrals for the survivor to access all the possible support. I was at the centre of all of this, and it was not a walk in the park.

Investigating and prosecuting domestic violence was also a major challenge. Our norms, religious and cultural biases affected the ability of the police to treat reported cases. There was a low level of prosecution of domestic violence cases. The issue of it being 'domestic' – 'husband and wife' matter posed serious challenges. It negatively impacted the attitude of some officers towards such incidents.

Over the years, I have been privileged to train over two hundred police officers at different fora on the provisions of the Protection Against Domestic Violence, 2007 Law, and it was always remarkable the pushback I would receive from the officers.

'Madam Lola, this is Africa, are you telling me that I should ask the man to leave the house? I can't do that,' a police officer under training once said.

I could feel his voice trembling; I could feel the weight of culture wrap itself around his voice like a boa constrictor. I made to answer him but he added,

'Madam Lola, officers of the police are not here to break homes o, the best we can do is to advise the parties, we have been doing that, and it has been working.'

Not wanting to sound dismissing 'I know but would you rather the woman dies in that husband's house?' I asked, askance.

'Madam Lola, the Bible says…' he paused, then continued 'I can't do that again o, my boss put me in the guard room after the husband petitioned me for detaining him on account of Domestic Violence.'

'Me too, I have my own problem with my husband, every marriage has challenges, my husband cheats on me too, is that enough for me to leave my marriage?' added someone else.

These responses obviously were discouraging, but instructive. It is not that these officers did not know what to do. After all, such cases could be treated the same way as the offences of Assault occasioning harm. What was stopping them from doing the needful was our culture and religion.

Indeed, *culture could eat strategy for breakfast.* Some of them could not bring themselves to do what they were supposed to do, despite knowing the tenets of the law.

Therefore, it was obvious why we were achieving a low success rate in prosecuting domestic violence cases. Some police officers would even actively discourage, and some would refuse, outright, to file the survivor incident as a case at the station.

Some would not, at the least, call the alleged abuser; rather, they would insist that the survivor returns to the place of abuse. It was in exceptional circumstances that some would be *magnanimous* enough to refer the survivor to a health facility. Even at that, nothing concrete was done. In the few times, the alleged abuser would be *invited* to the station, nothing tangible would come of it.

Rather, the alleged abuser would be asked to *beg* his wife. Many a time, the abuser leaves the police station even more emboldened. Or the parties would be asked to *go and come back.* This could happen over a period of a month. This is usually done, with the hopes that the extended family would intervene, and the issue would have been resolved. This was, and to a certain extent remains, a major challenge—the response by certain police officers to domestic violence.

The lack of adequate funding to investigate Sexual and Gender-Based Violence cases remains a major challenge and an inhibitor of access to justice. Approximately 95% of Gender Desks or Family Support Units do not have vehicles attached to their units nor do they have appropriate running cost for their offices to function, and yet they are expected to conduct detailed investigations, when they lack the financial capacity to do so. The financial burden is heavily centred on the victim.

The victim mobilises the police to investigate the case, effect arrest, duplicate the case file, transport the suspect and the police to the court and in some instances pay for the suspect to be transported to the correctional facility after being remanded by the court.

The victim is literally paying to get justice. This in itself is doubly traumatic. Justice becomes elusive, and that's why some survivors would say 'I don't have money to do case' not because they do not want to get justice for themselves or for their children, but because they do not have the funds to pursue justice.

In my early years, when my enthusiasm was fresh and coloured with inexperience, I would always accompany survivors of sexual abuse to the police station and then to the court where the suspect was ordered to be remanded. I witnessed the different non-receipted payments that had to be made at the different stages.

As much as I was always surprised, I could not begrudge the officers as they were not allocated funds for investigation of the case. It was left to the survivor to fund their case. Afterall, they are the ones who want justice. This remains one of the main reasons why people fallout from the criminal justice system. Access to Justice is a luxury that some people cannot afford.

For health, we had similar challenges in survivors of sexual violence accessing free, quality health care services. Prior to the establishment of Mirabel Centre, most victims received support from the General Hospitals or at the Health Centres, but at a cost. Furthermore, services that were being rendered were not holistic in nature.

Contrary to what is now obtainable, most survivors were not able to access psychosocial support. Therefore, while they were physically cared for, their mental health needs were not being addressed.

We also had capacity challenges which were evident during the documentation of cases by the doctors. Clients were not receiving head-to-toe forensic examinations, also the documentation was not as detailed as it should have been.

The issue of confidentiality was also a great concern as the medical reports were easily accessible. We had instances where medical reports were used as a bargaining chip for settling cases out of court. This situation was not ideal and was not in keeping up with best practices. Then, like the miracle of water in a wilderness, Mirabel Centre came to show us what should be done. Mirabel Centre epitomises best practices in providing survivor-centred medical care for sexual assault survivors. Their model places the survivor at the centre. It ensures that survivors are believed, and have the confidence to regain their voice. This is made possible through the provision of psychosocial support not only for the victim-survivors but for their families as well.

Still, one centre to service, the entire metropolis was not sustainable. To this end, mainstreaming Gender- Based Violence, a public health concern became a priority.

CHAPTER 6

TACKLING SEXUAL AND GENDERBASED VIOLENCE AS A PUBLIC HEALTH CONCERN

When we started DSVRT, ensuring access to quality health care was a major factor, especially for survivors of sexual violence. Survivors need immediate and free medical assistance and at that time, Mirabel Centre, the first sexual assault referral centre in Nigeria was barely a year old. Mirabel centre showed us what was possible; they provided emergency medical and psychosocial support at zero cost to survivors of sexual violence.

Mirabel Centre was, and still is the model for the provision of sexual assault management services to survivors. Survivors are treated by competent personnel with dignity and empathy and they are at the centre of the process. They are heard, believed, and supported on their road to healing.

When we began operations, all our information, education and communication materials had details of Mirabel Centre on them. In fact, some people thought that Mirabel was owned or funded by the Government at that time.

Despite the amazing work being done by Mirabel Centre, the need for government to drive and own this process became ever more compelling. The existence of only one specialised centre in the whole of Lagos was not sustainable.

I was not oblivious to the strain, both physically and financially placed on victims to journey from far places to a particular location. Perhaps, it is also borne out of my belief that government should as much as possible, be the chief provider of basic services. The government's social contract with its citizenry must be upheld in ensuring adequate provision of services, including healthcare. The provision of quality and affordable healthcare, to me, was not a luxury, let alone one that survivors could not afford.

The situation did not augur well with me. I felt we could do better. We could empower our institutions, especially the Primary Healthcare Centres which are close to the people, in the communities. Access to medical care should truly be accessible. And so again, I resorted to what was in existence. During this inception stage, I did a lot of research, I had to.

I was literally learning on the job. There was no blueprint to follow. Unfortunately, we found out that we did not have a Sexual Assault Standing Order in the country. Neither did we have trained, specialised skilled health workers who could provide a forensic medical examination on survivors of sexual violence in both our primary and secondary health facilities at that time.

For this to work, we decided to commence in phases, and approach the Primary Healthcare Centres first before scaling up to the general hospitals. The selection of the PHCs was very strategic. They are closer to the community; the provision of medical treatment was already at a subsidised price and for various reasons, the PHCs were not as overwhelmed with patients as the General Hospitals. This was strange to me.

We were also looking at ways the local police stations could work closely with the closest health facility to them, for ease of referrals, expedited collection and preservation of evidence, and immediate medical attention for survivors that were present at the police station.

I will always be grateful to Mrs Ibidunni Alakija-Ladapo. After pitching the idea of starting with the PHCs to her, she advised that we bring in donors, including UNAIDS, UNFPA to assist in this process as well as provide technical support in drafting the standing order.

In view of the magnitude of this proposed reform, an approval had to be sought from the Governor. We wanted an approval to upgrade primary healthcare centres to the status of Sexual Assault Referral Centres, to provide sexual assault management services and medication at no cost to the survivor. At that time, there were no Sexual Assault Evidence Collection Kits (referred to as Rape Kits) in Lagos State and indeed, in Nigeria. We therefore, sought to use this opportunity to also procure rape kits to make this a total and holistic project.

Mrs Omotola Rotimi, *(a General* I cannot go to war without), who was the then Director, Office of Public Defender had previously reached out to me about the need to leverage forensics in solving sexual violence cases.

I remember she had designed a prototype rape kit. The different items were kept in a red shoe box to emphasise the thickness of the box. This action made the idea even more tangible as I could now conceptualise what we wanted to achieve.

While we did not have comprehensive statistics on sexual violence, we however leveraged statistics from the Mirabel Centre in ascertaining trends and areas of prevalence which assisted us in the pilot phase of the project.

We eventually got approval from the Governor to embark on the upgrade of Primary Healthcare Centres and develop the Standing Order. Approval was also secured to procure the first batch of Rape Kits. Imagine my excitement. This was finally happening. The State was taking ownership of this. This was an awesome moment to be alive.

The next set of events that would follow the approval were very illuminating. Until that moment, I had never done anything directly with the health sector; the workings of the Primary Healthcare Board, the establishments, internal protocols, and policies for engaging with the Board and the medical workers. As with most innovations, there would always be some pushbacks or resistance to change. Sometimes, it even appeared that the project was being deliberately frustrated. I would therefore always be grateful and indebted to Dr Ibironke Sodeinde, the then Permanent Secretary, Primary Healthcare Board. Also, I appreciate Dr Veronica Iwayemi and Dr Okaga (ma soeur francaise) for their support in making this a reality. These amazing women believed in this innovation, and ensured it became a success against all odds.

Introducing an initiative to an organisation you don't have control over and expecting total acceptance or full embracement is a steep mountain to climb, so I learnt that for such to be successful, everybody must be carried along. Everybody has to have a sense of belonging; they must be involved in the process and the planning phase. You must make them see the role they play in the success or otherwise of the initiative so that they will be able to own it. On Thursday, 25 February 2016, we launched this great project. It was surreal. The sleepless nights and last-minute changes had finally paid off. However, the real work was just beginning, and I knew it. Even if every other person was oblivious of this, I wasn't. I clutched it firmly to my heart, I cradled it in my palm, because, that was what it needed—to be nurtured and nursed until full bloom.

Unfortunately, shortly after we rolled out the pilot phase, Dr Sodeinde retired from public service. There was also a change in leadership at the Board as Dr Sanni, who was then the Director of Medical Services, had also been posted out. We, therefore, had to start building a relationship with the new Permanent Secretary and other members of management.

In hindsight, maybe these are some of the reasons attributable to the slow implementation of the project at the PHC. We struggled to get it up and running. We also had to alter the original design which was to identify five comprehensive Primary Healthcare Centres in the IBILE (Ikeja, Badagry, Ikorodu, and Lagos and Epe) axis to serve as the pilot. Regarding the distribution of kits, priority would be given to these pilot facilities. However, the response we got from the Board was that all the 57 comprehensive PHCs in the state should be included in the implementation stage.

And so we had upgraded pilot comprehensive Primary Healthcare Centres, developed the Lagos State Standing Order which was ratified by the Hon. Commissioner for Health, procured Sexual Assault Evidence Collection Kits, designed Medical reports and relevant forms as well as referral cards for the health facilities, designed posters, and then commenced community engagement with a view to increasing awareness about this new initiative.

However, there was an area I hadn't thought of. If we wanted people to embrace this initiative, it had to be free. The provision of drugs, routine tests medical examination, documentation, follow-up care, everything had to be free. It would come at absolutely no cost to the victims. Whilst the doctors would provide *free* medical examination, the tests, the drugs and other support services had to be paid for.

To this end, we enumerated the different routine tests, and for sexual assault victims, we came up with the following: pregnancy test, blood grouping (to narrow suspects), HIV test (free already), venereal Disease Research Laboratory Test (Syphilis). HVs, Semen Micro Culture and Sens, Hepatitis B, vaginal swab, and urine microscopy.

After consultation with the Ministry of Health, Dr Olajide Idris, Hon. Commissioner for Health and Dr Olufemi Onanuga, Special Adviser on Primary Health Care; the Ministry graciously approved a subsidised amount for these tests. However, the issue of who would pay the subsidised amount had not yet been addressed.

There was another hurdle to cross. Some of these tests could not be conducted at the Primary Healthcare Centre level (VDR and HVS), so we had to seek approval to refer the samples collected for such tests to the closest General Hospitals for analysis at a subsidised amount. This was also graciously approved by the Ministry. This process was facilitated by Mrs Adeola Birch in the Ministry of Health.

While we had secured major approvals, I could not celebrate yet because unfortunately, we did not have any provision for payment of these tests, even at a subsidised amount in the running cost for my office.

On 26 April 2016, two months after the launch, I approached the then Attorney General, Mr Adeniji Kazeem, informing him of our challenge. He advised that a letter be written to Northwest Petroleum Plc. requesting their financial support in this regard.

A week later, Mr Kazeem called me into his office to inform me that Northwest Petroleum had decided to financially support this initiative. I remember immediately going on my knees in appreciation. I did not concern myself with the fact that he had guests in his office. One might even think the funds were intended for my personal use. I felt a huge burden had been lifted. It appeared that everything had fallen into place. I proposed that the funds be domiciled at the Primary Healthcare Centre Board, and accessible on a reimbursement basis by the health facilities after providing medical treatment to survivors. Gratefully, this was accepted.

From the inception of the vision, there were so many challenges that appeared insurmountable. At one point, I just felt like giving up. Perhaps because there was no blueprint to follow, we were literally making it all up as we went ahead.

The provision of funds now meant survivors that are present at the designated PHCs would be able to receive care at no cost. Indubitably, as with every new policy, it took a while before the key stakeholders became accustomed to the initiative in its entirety.

We had instances where survivors would pay for a medication after being examined, and when brought to our attention, we would ensure the funds were refunded to the client. Despite this, we kept re-emphasising the fact that survivors were not supposed to part with their money.

As we proceeded with implementing this initiative, I noticed that there was still a lacuna that had not yet been addressed, which was the provision of psychosocial support at the health centres and the hospitals. We were desirous of ensuring survivors receive holistic medical support including psychosocial support, hence the need to empower nurses to provide psychosocial support and services. To make this a reality, a Standard Operating Procedure was developed for nurses on providing psychosocial support to survivors of domestic and sexual violence.

The aim of the Standing Order was to, amongst other things, equip health care providers, particularly, nurses and medical social workers with relevant tools to provide psychosocial therapy, support and management of domestic and sexual assault patients, and provide standards for the provision of health care and collection of forensic evidence for sexual assault survivors.

This, in our view, would facilitate examination and management of patients after domestic and sexual assault, and improve the quality and documentation of evidence collection. It was also of utmost importance that nurses at both primary and secondary care levels of the healthcare system (providing support to domestic and sexual assault patients) be able to recognise physical and sexual assault document pertinent history, provide psychological support, and refer to appropriate agencies.

Through this policy, nurses and medical social workers would therefore be the first port of call for survivors. History would be taken, and provision of psychosocial support would take place before the survivor is medically examined. Furthermore, client care management and follow up care would be designed for each survivor.

We were most fortunate to have support from Ford Foundation for this initiative. I would always be grateful to Dr Victoria Omoera; Ministry of Health and Dr Veronica Iwayemi; Primary Healthcare Board, for their unwavering support, commitment, and dedication in ensuring that this initiative was fully implemented.

This was a turning point and a learning opportunity for me. Once again, it showed me how much progress can be made when the right people are in the right position as decision makers in government. Nothing is impossible, and everything falls into place.

Since then, a lot of strides have been made. The Ministry of Health has owned this process in ensuring that General Hospitals in Lagos State were upgraded to provide sexual assault management services. Similarly, the General Hospitals have also been equipped with Sexual Assault Evidence Collection Kits.

Another remarkable achievement was the establishment of the Sexual Intervention Fund, spearheaded by the Lagos State Health Management Agency (LASHMA) with support from Her Excellency, the First Lady of

Lagos State, Dr (Mrs) Claudiana Ibijoke Sanwo-Olu. This was a laudable initiative geared towards ensuring that victims can receive immediate comprehensive care at no cost in all the government hospitals and some selected private hospitals.

By virtue of this initiative, survivors who become pregnant as a result of sexual assault, and are desirous of keeping the pregnancy can receive antenatal care at no cost. Similarly, the cost of delivery of the child would be borne by the state, and postnatal care would also be provided. In the unfortunate instance where the survivor suffers tears, and requires reconstructive surgeries, such cost would also be borne by the state.

The aim was to alleviate the sufferings and lift e the financial burden of the aftermath of sexual assault on the survivor. This is a great instance in which policy has a direct, positive impact on the people.

Comparing how we begun to the pioneering initiatives that have been implemented so far, I am certainly excited for what the future holds for Lagos State in tackling Sexual and Gender-Based Violence as a health concern.

PHARMACIES

In the wake of the COVID-19 Pandemic in 2020 and the complete restriction of movement that followed, I was really worried for survivors of domestic violence who were prevented from visiting the hospitals, especially as some people dreaded hospitals during that period. I recall a particular case that was reported which I handled, I asked the lady if she had sustained injuries after the violence and she said she had some bruises on her chest and the left part of her face.

The details of the closest Primary Health Centre were given to her so she could receive medical attention and assist in building her case. Unfortunately, she did not go, rather she went to her nearby pharmacy where she purchased pain reliefs. According to her, she didn't want the stress of going to the hospital. She added that after previous abuses, she would always go to a pharmacy.

Unfortunately for this particular client, she did not want this case to be reported to the police station, but she wanted mediation to be deployed, and she would then state that she was no longer interested in the union and wanted to be separated for an undisclosed period of time.

During the virtual mediation, the spouse denied being abusive. In fact, he said he wished he had had our number that he should be the one reporting violence. As is customary in such instances where evidence is absent, we can only at best use persuasive authority to assist the client in getting some of the reliefs being sought.

After handling the case, I had a moment to reflect on the case in particular and other cases we had handled during COVID-19. The lockdown also afforded me the opportunity to identify areas we were struggling with, where we were thriving and opportunities that existed for sustainable changes.

Very few survivors of domestic violence actually have real evidence to corroborate their assertions. Real evidence can include pictorial evidence, medical evidence, police reports, or any documentation that basically gives credence to their allegations and assertions. I also remembered the fact that some survivors of Domestic Violence I was privileged to engage would tell me that after the violent incident, they visited the pharmacy for pain relief, but did not go to the police station or hospital to report.

And then it hit me, why are we not partnering with the Pharmacy Council in Nigeria? It would be ideal that once a survivor visits a pharmacy, particularly at a community licensed pharmacy, before any medication is prescribed, certain questions are asked and an index of suspicion would trigger some insight and if violence is disclosed, the client is referred appropriately.

Is it also not possible for the pharmacists that attended to the client to also write a note, documenting their findings and what necessitated the purchase of drugs in the first place? Wouldn't it be great if the pharmacist, with the consent of the client could activate the referral pathway once a case is reported and ensure the survivor can access the various services, including emergency services, police, legal, psychosocial support? If the pharmacist simply dials the DSVRT toll free line, these services would be made available to the victim and they would be informed of options available. The community pharmacy at that point then becomes a safe space for victims.

While contemplating who would be the best person to assist in making this a reality, Pharm. Shakirat Adeosun; Director of Pharmaceutical Services at the Primary Healthcare Board came, to mind. We had worked together when we were implementing the upgrading of PHCs to provide sexual assault management services. Indeed, she was a great ally.

I reached out to her and gave her a brief synopsis of the problem and how we wanted to address it. When I haven't yet spoken, she completed my sentences; she understood ahead what we were desirous of doing. She intimated me of partnerships that needed to be explored, meetings that had to be scheduled with the Pharmaceutical Council of Nigeria, (Lagos Branch). She highlighted that the Chairman of Pharmaceutical Society of Nigeria, Lagos Branch, the Chairperson of female pharmacies, and the Chairman of Licensed Community Pharmacists were key stakeholders, and their acceptance of the innovation was necessary.

On our part, we developed the policy document, which included a step-by-step guide of making use of the code scheme and a booklet on what Domestic Violence entailed as well as the Tool Kit to facilitate this process. Posters which would be displayed in the pharmacies were also designed, as well as prescription sheets for distribution to partnering community licensed pharmacists.

My colleagues in the office, Rhodiyat Ogbara, Tumininu Oni and I brainstormed on the best approach. Would it be training for pilot pharmacists? Would our focus be community pharmacists or would it be a general sensitisation? Especially bearing in mind that there were no readily accessible funds for this initiative.

It was decided that we would do both. Besides developing the policy document, there would also be the need to ensure residents are informed about this novel service that can be accessed at the pharmacies.

And that was how *Speak to INU* (I need you) was birthed. We commenced by entering into a Memorandum of Understanding with the Pharmaceutical Council of Nigeria, Lagos Branch, highlighting the responsibilities of both parties. This was an initiative that the leadership of the Council, particularly the Chairman, Pharm. Gbolagade Iyola, as well as the Chairman of the Community Licensed Pharmacists, Pharm. Lawrence Ekhator, were most supportive of.

During the time of commencement of the initiative, over one hundred and fifty (150) community licensed pharmacists had signed up to the scheme, and had been trained on the application of the *Speak to INU* code scheme.

CHAPTER 7

MUCH ADO ABOUT PUBLIC POLICY

Before delving into the realm of providing support to victims of Sexual and Gender-Based Violence, I had over five years' experience in proposing policies. I had worked on the Badia East Resettlement Action Plan, Lagos State Scholarship Board, the Crime Data Register, reviewed extension of maternity leave policy for public servants to six months and introduction of the paternity leave into the State Public Service Rules (Lagos was the first to achieve this), the provision of pro bono services through the Lagos Public Interest Law Partnership scheme, etc. I had also been privileged to sit on law reform committees instrumental in the enactment of the Criminal Law of Lagos State, 2011, Tenancy Law, Customary Law as well as the Magistrate Courts Law.

I was therefore very much aware of the potency and efficacy of policies. Policy demonstrates the intention, and direction of an institution. It shows the vision in a codified document. It also demonstrates political will to address an issue of governance.

Between September and December 2014, barely three (3) months after the DSVRT was inaugurated, I was considering our first policy document. During my research into the setting up of the team, I came across the need for a Sex Offenders Register. This Register was to primarily ensure that the identities of all sex convicts were captured; this included their names, aliases, biometrics, last known addresses, passport photos, etc. Similarly, the register enrolled into a database which was usually accessible by the Police, the Judiciary and the prosecution.

While at that time, there wasn't a conclusive research on the efficacy of the Register in preventing the occurrence of Sexual and Gender-Based Violence, I discussed with Mr Akingbolahan Adeniran on the need to have a Sex Offenders Register. Mr Adeniran suggested that we should reach out to his colleagues in other jurisdictions to share practical insights into the operations of the sex offenders register in their respective jurisdictions.

We were particularly interested in ascertaining the timing of the inclusion of a convicted person's name in the register giving the possibility of appeals. He wrote to Julien Savoye to share the perspective of France as well as Jeff Ansell for England's. Part of the response we received from Jeff Ansell was that the Sex Offenders Register is not a public document and a sex convict's inclusion or otherwise on it requires a court order to be made public.

Mr Adeniran's colleague in America informed us that they have two kinds of reporting requirements. While there is a register that each state maintains, they also require offenders to register in any neighbourhood they move to; we were also informed that failing to register is a criminal offence because it allows them to track the location of offenders. According to Julien, France did not publicise their register, nor have such public records. According to him, the disadvantages that come with such records—loss of dignity, public shaming and their consequences on the life of convicts, who are already punished through other means—are seen as outweighing the advantages of making the public aware of the identity of sexual offenders.

This provided a lot of clarity. Although we could not monitor sex offenders upon their release after serving time, we could not publish their names without having legislative backing either. What was being proposed was an Executive Order, seeking a way to compile a list of all sex offenders in Lagos State, as much as the constitution allowed us to.

It should be reiterated here that the major aim of the Sex Offenders' Monitoring Programme is to reduce repeat cases by providing names and personal details of convicted sex offenders in the state to a central database. The Database will be accessible to individuals and organisations with an established need for the information.

For example, school proprietors who want to do staff recruitment could access this Register to carry out background checks on applicants. It is believed that this would serve as a deterrent and also help potential victims to protect themselves from known and nearby sex offenders by facilitating public monitoring and preventing known criminals from being placed in a position of opportunity to commit further sex offences.

Initially, the policy being developed was supposed to be limited to establishing the Sex Offenders Register; however, an opportunity came up for expansion. During that same time when the Executive Order was being conceptualised, we welcomed our partners from International Senior Lawyers Project, United Kingdom, who had recently concluded a training course for lawyers in the Ministry of Justice. This had been organised by the Office of the Attorney General and so we had a send forth dinner for them.

During the dinner, I spoke to one of the facilitators about the proposal to establish a Sex Offenders Register, and during our conversation, he asked if we had a mandated reporting policy. According to him, in America, certain officers that worked with children are mandated to report actual or suspected incidents of abuse. At that time, to the best of my knowledge, there was no such policy in Lagos or even in Nigeria.

Another opportunity to conduct a research on an interesting area had presented itself. In Lagos, we had already enacted the Child's Rights Law, the embodiment of all rights and responsibilities of children and all institutions legally empowered to provide services to children. It was however most expedient to have an executive directive making it compulsory for all State School Administrators, Counsellors, Teachers, Social Welfare Officers and any other official of the State Government having any dealings with children to report any suspected or actual child abuse or neglect to the relevant authorities.

Those officers were identified primarily because of the critical roles they play in observing children. This was particularly true in the schools as children spend on average six hours in the school premises every day of the week. Teachers, guidance counsellors and school administrators are in a vantage position in detecting signs of abuse. It was important that they be awakened to their roles in ensuring the safety of children in their care.

Accordingly, I added the Mandated Reporting policy into the draft Executive Order on the Sex Offenders Register, hoping it would sail through. As usual, I approached Mr Adeniran, and then it was presented to the Attorney General for approval and onward submission to the Governor for ratification. Mr Ipaye agreed with the provision and the Executive Order draft which had now been titled Sex Offenders Register and Mandated Reporting Programme was submitted via a Memorandum to the Governor for approval and ratification.

A couple of days later, I was working late in the evening, as it was our custom then, when Mr Ipaye called me to say that he was on his way back to the office, but he wanted to let me know that the Governor had treated the Memorandum approving the executive Order. Also, he wanted to publicly sign the Executive Order, the same way he would assent to a Law. My joy knew no bounds.

After getting off the call, I rushed to my colleague, Mr Adeniran, beaming with excitement. We celebrated briefly, by that time, Mr Ipaye had returned to the office. He instructed that members of DSVRT, relevant Non-Governmental Organisations as well as civil society organisations be invited to attend the public signing.

On the 1st of December, 2014, Mr Babatunde Raji Fashola, SAN, publicly signed the Executive Order on the Sex Offenders Register and Mandated Reporting Programme. History was made. We were the first state in the country to have a codified legal framework on the Sex Offenders Register and Mandated Reporting programme. It was indeed a great day. It was also the beginning of great networks established. The amazing individuals I met are: Mrs Lola Alonge, Executive Director, Child Health Advocacy Initiative; and representatives from Child Protection Network, FOMWAN, and UNICEF. We now had a policy, but we had to ensure that it was implemented fully especially the Mandated Reporting Programme. It was important to empower officers with relevant information on their role as Mandated Reporters, signs to look out for if they suspected abuse, and how to report concerns upon receipt of disclosures of abuse from children. To that effect, I prepared a draft Manual on Mandated Reporting as well as a reporting form that we expected would be used in all child-centred institutions.

The manual emphasised the legal standard for reporting—when there was *reasonable cause* to suspect abuse or neglect. This was an extremely low threshold that meant that once there was reasonable suspicion of abuse, the same should be reported immediately. The manual also provided confidentiality, different forms of abuse, red flags to look out for and reporting obligations.

Given the multi-sectorial dimension approach we had introduced, the draft manual was shared with the Ministry of Education and the Office of Youth and Social Development for their comments and contributions. Once we received their contributions, the document was finalised.

At that time, we still did not have a budget, neither did we have any resources to embark on the various child protection trainings for the Mandated Reporters and also, empower children with information about Child Abuse, their rights, and signs to look out for. After all, children have a role to play in their own protection.

Mr Ipaye directed that a memorandum seeking funds to actualise the above activities be prepared for the Governor's approval and the same was done. The memo came back approved, and we commenced internal processes for accessing the funds. This ushered me into the practice of seeking approval and the paperwork and processes that would follow before the funds were released.

At the same time, I typed various letters of sponsorship to numerous companies, and Mr Ipaye would sign each letter, he would encourage me to follow up. However, we were now approaching the end of Mr Babatunde Raji Fashola's administration and unfortunately, we could not access the approved funds. Nevertheless, we could re-present the memorandum for validation. Eventually, it was approved by Governor Ambode. This was the first approval we received with financial implications.

With this approval, we commenced our Child Protection trainings for guidance counsellors, school social workers, teachers, school administrators, Heads of School, etc.

I had the opportunity of working with child protection experts like Mr Taiwo Akinlami, Mrs Lola Alonge, Mrs Modupeola Sahid Adebambo and Dr Babajide Martins who all served as facilitators for the training. Over the years, we have been able to build capacity of over 6,000 professionals in school institutions on child protection concerns and their role as mandated reporters.

While ensuring full implementation of the Executive Order on mandated reporting, we realised that it was important to concurrently engage parents and children themselves.

This, in my view, was a proactive approach. Empowering parents with information about child rights, child abuse, signs to look out for if they suspected abuse, enlightening them about the process of grooming, etc. We believed that this would help reduce the likelihood of their children being abused. And so, we entered into partnership with the Parents Teachers Forum intending to organise parents' association conferences, to take place on Saturdays.

At the same time, we had started our partnership with a non-governmental organisation, Rubies Ink, founded by Esther Ijewere to empower children via the College Acquaintance Rape Education (CARE) initiative.

To ensure all members of the response team could participate in this initiative, we divided ourselves by districts and all members at some point or the other were part of imparting knowledge, fellowshipping, and inspiring children across the state.

Through this partnership with Rubies Ink, we engaged over 3000 primary and secondary school students, drawn from over 50 schools in the state. To properly monitor and evaluate our effectiveness, we leveraged the six education districts in the state. With the success of the initiative, it was clear we had to scale up the activities. And that was how the Safeguarding the Rights of a Child (STRAC) initiative was born.

Asides from engaging children through interactive workshops, I thought it would be good to have an informative, colourful book that would illustrate the message on body safety, child rights, child abuse, and steps to take to report abuse. And so, I came up with a narrative and shared with an illustrator to help bring the story to life. When we had the first draft, I shared it with members of the team and the contributions and comments were reflected. The draft was updated, and we were ready to print.

I remember when Mr Abayomi Olusola Sunday (life saver, printer extraordinaire) handed over a copy of the Safeguarding the Rights of a Child book for children to me, I resembled a field of golden daffodils swaying in windy joy. It is such a blessing to be able to handle what you have conceptualised in your mind. The reality came with a priceless feeling. I recall showing the copy to some children for their input, since they were our targeted audience. Their feedback was important to us. Since that day, we have gone ahead to print over 20,000 copies of STRAC which have been distributed across the state.

Despite our progress, Lagos State did not have a Child Protection Policy in place. This was not acceptable or satisfactory. And so, on 15 June 2015, a memorandum was written to the Governor informing him of the gap in our system and the need for a policy to be developed.

This was particularly hinged on the convention on the Rights of the Child, which Nigeria has ratified was adopted and opened for signature, ratification and accession by the United Nations General Assembly resolution 44/25 of 20 November 1989. Article 4 clearly states that government has a duty to ensure that children are adequately protected and those minimum standards, including Child Protection policies are adequately provided for. The ratification of this Convention was what gave rise to the enactment of the Child's Rights Act 2003 and the subsequent enactment of the Lagos State Child's Rights Law, 2007.

Fortunately, Governor Akinwunmi Ambode approved this, and we set to work. In January 2016, a subcommittee was constituted, comprising representatives from the Ministry of Youth and Social Development, Mrs Laide Latinwo; Late Mrs Kehinde Idowu, Ministry of Women Affairs and Poverty Alleviation; Mrs Alaba Fadairo, Ministry of Education; Mrs Busola Agagu, Ministry of Health; Dr Okunnu, Mrs Roseleen Akinroye, representative of United Nations International Children's Emergency Fund, (UNICEF), Mr Taiwo Akinlami of Taiwo Akinlami Academy, Mrs Lola Alonge of Child Health Advocacy Initiative, Mrs Yemi Ebulu Eyuntari of Saffron SDG, Inspector Emegwamor Kenneth Okafor of the Nigeria Police Force and my humble self.

To be more efficient, we outlined the objectives of the sub-committee on child protection and safeguarding to include: enhance synergy between all the responder agencies, clearly define roles of the different responder agencies and train responder agencies on their respective roles in responding to child abuse, maltreatment and neglect. We also highlighted their responsibilities and deliverables to include: development of a Protocol on Multi Agency Response to Child Protection and Safeguarding the rights of a child (clear definition of roles), embarkment on trainings for social workers, counsellors, teachers, health officials and the Nigeria Police on Child protection, development of a Child Protection and Safeguarding policy to be implemented by the state (especially at the schools), identification and putting together of an advocacy campaign for the year and making recommendations to strengthen the respective agencies.

The first deliverable we decided to focus on was developing a Child Protection Policy. We had our first meeting on the 26 February 2016 in the Conference Room of the Ministry of Youth and Social Development. We had a draft Child protection document which I prepared and we also had the advantage of the Child Protection Policy which had been recently formulated by the Federal Government. Mrs Roseleen Akinroye of UNICEF was kind enough to avail the Committee of a copy. We were then able to compare the two documents and members provided insights from our different perspectives.

We believed that a Child Protection Policy was necessary to encourage all agencies, organisations and community members to give priority to the protection of children as a shared responsibility. The policy is a catalyst for the awareness and commitment of all parties, including every member of the community involved in the protection of children.

To ensure that the rights of children are adequately safeguarded and protected, the policy would apply to all state government organisations, schools, child-centred structures, orphanages and child related institutions located in the state, and institutions and organisations in the state's public and private sectors, both formal and informal. Key stakeholders include: line ministries, Lagos State Safety Commission, Lagos State Quality Assurance Bureau, Department of Private Education, employers/employees and prospective employers/ employees from the public and private sectors, both formal and informal in the State etc.

The policy also refers to safe recruitments of staff. This is of utmost importance as several cases of sexual abuse of children are being carried out by school staff, including teachers and bus drivers. It is therefore necessary that structures are in place to ensure the safe recruitment of staff in all child centred organisations.

As regards training of staff, all organisations are responsible for ensuring that their staff and volunteers working with children access and receive regular training to equip them with skills and knowledge for the purpose of understanding, identifying, and responding to child protection issues. On our own part as the government, we are mandated to continue to improve capacity of all responder agencies.

The policy also refers to Serious Case Reviews (SCR). This would be done by the Maternal Perinatal Death Surveillance Report Committee, currently chaired by the Ministry of Health. This Review will take place where a child dies (including death by suicide) and abuse or neglect is known or suspected to be a factor in their death.

The purpose of the Serious Case Review is to find out if there are any lessons to be learned from the case about how local professionals and agencies work together to safeguard and promote the welfare of children, identify what those lessons are, how they will be acted on and what is expected to change because of the serious case review and improve interagency working to better safeguard and promote the welfare of children.

This sub-committee which was chaired by Mrs Latinwo comprised of committed and passionate child protection experts. We worked without any budget or seating allowance, as, unfortunately, there was no budget for this. It just epitomised the fact that passion and the desire to ensure all children in Lagos State were safe was and continues to remain our utmost priority.

During one of our meetings, Mrs Ebulu-Eyuntari suggested that the component of Safeguarding should be more pronounced in our draft. She was very passionate about safeguarding which, in her view was all encompassing and all the members agreed with her position.

We were therefore tasked to conduct a research on safeguarding and incorporate same into the document. After several meetings, on 23 April 2016 we finally shared a draft policy document with sub-committee members for their input. The draft document was also shared with the entire team for their input. Upon receipt of the various contributions, the draft policy was presented to the Hon. Attorney General for circulation to the respective heads of ministries and institutions for their comments.

While we were waiting to receive the comments from all the stakeholders, at that time, I was not satisfied that the document should just be a policy. My mind flashed back to the Executive Order on Sex Offenders Register, and I felt perhaps, we could use that similar vehicle to achieve our instant purpose. I expressed my concerns to Mrs Omotilewa Ibirogba who agreed. She also wanted a document that the governor could endorse. The issue now was could a governor sign a policy? Isn't that what commissioners were supposed to do? We were not sure if we would be offending any rule if the governor were to sign this policy document.

I reached out to Mr Adeniran who was now working in the Office of the Vice President. He advised that even though policies are generally signed by commissioners, we would not be offending any rule if the governor signed it. Rather, it would be reinforcing the fact that the state government was fully committed to the protection of children in the state.

We decided to go with the policy bearing in mind that we already obtained approval from the governor in this regard.

We had requested that the governor publicly signed the Policy. The date was fixed for 13 June 2016 at 2 p.m. We had sent out letters of invitation to all our partners. Heads of Development partners had been notified. The Commissioner of Police, CP Fatai Owoseni, had also been invited.

We, together with other invited stakeholders, arrived at the Governor's office and we were waiting to be ushered in for the signing ceremony. We had been waiting for approximately an hour after the event was supposed to take place when I received a text message from an unknown number that read, 'signing has been cancelled'. I didn't understand what was happening.

All my attempts to reach the person who sent the text proved abortive. I did not understand what was going on. Finally, a colleague who had come out of the Governor's office approached our delegation and informed us that the signing had been postponed indefinitely.

I had to start apologising to our invited participants. I could not even give any reassurance as to if it would be signed at a later date. We all walked out of the Governor's office, disappointed, but most of all, uncertain. I was heartbroken.

I remember returning to the office, and waiting till my boss would return from the Executive Council meeting, to get information first hand from him as to what went wrong. He said the general consensus was that some people opined that we already had a Child's Rights Law, some didn't think it was appropriate for the governor to sign a policy document, and some were of the opinion that it should be a draft piece of legislation and some felt that the concerned commissioners could sign the policy.

The bottom line was that it was not going to sail through at the time, and so came the onus for me to research into the need for the Child Protection Policy and advise accordingly.

That night, as I was returning home, I felt heavy and damp as though I draped on a million wet blankets. After my whole family had slept, I curled up on the sofa and sobbed like a lost child. I remembered all the hard work that had been put in by the sub-committee members. I remembered that during most of this period, I was on maternity leave, and yet I was still coming in for the meetings. It appeared all the sacrifices weren't worth it.

Nonetheless, after reflecting on the day, I opened my laptop and began the research to provide more ammunition. The issue of the need for a policy had to be addressed.

I realised that the Convention on the Rights of the Child, which Nigeria has ratified and adopted particularly Article 4, clearly states that government has a duty to ensure that children are adequately protected and those minimum standards, including Child Protection policies are adequately provided for. The ratification of this Convention was what gave rise to the enactment of the Child's Rights Act 2003 and the subsequent enactment of the Lagos State Child's Rights Law, 2007. This law and other legislative enactments informed the need for the formulation of the Safeguarding and Child Protection Programme.

Concerning the preferred vehicle that would be selected, the straightforward option would have been to formulate a Bill on Safeguarding and Child Protection. While it would be the most straightforward, it would definitely not be the quickest. And so, the option of Executive Order came up.

Executive Orders do not require legislative approval to take effect but they do have some legal weight. The Governor's source of authority to issue Executive Orders can be found in Part II, section 5 of the Constitution, which grants to the Governor the executive power. Section 5 further directs the State Governor to take care that the laws be faithfully executed.

Executive orders have the full force of law when they take authority from a legislative power which grants its power directly to the Executive by the Constitution. I argued that the importance of having the Child Protection and Safeguarding programme in the form of an Executive Order is primarily to make the programme binding on all State Child Centre structures—schools, crèches, hospitals, and for Primary Healthcare Centres to have a Safeguarding and Child Protection programme in their respective institutions.

Now, we are not able to mandate the private sector to adopt Child Protection programmes without a legislative enactment, the Executive Order would however be seen as a catalyst for the private sector to adopt similar programmes. The Government would also be seen as setting a good example for the private sector to emulate.

The importance of embracing this programme would be disseminated by having key stakeholders' interactions and incentives for private child-centred institutions in the State. As contemplated by the Safeguarding Programme, regular trainings would also be conducted to ensure improved capacity on how to handle issues of disclosure of abuse.

It was therefore proposed that the policy be converted into an Executive Order. This will give a stronger backing to the programme by imposing sanctions, limiting the discretion of numerous enforcement agencies, and most importantly ensuring immediate state-wide compliance. Some sanctions include the closure of institutions and the withdrawal of registration certificate. The proposed Executive Order would also create an enabling environment for compliance and make the implementation process quicker.

The following day, I discussed the above with Mrs Ibirogba, who agreed with this request to convert the policy into an Executive Order. She also suggested that we get expert advice from the Directorate of Legislative Drafting in the Ministry of Justice. I was able to speak to Mr David Kehinde (a skilled, cerebral draftsman) who assured me that we could make use of an Executive Order to achieve our purpose.

On this basis, the format was changed, and the policy would now become an attachment to the Executive Order. This afforded us the opportunity to include the implementing agencies. I thought this was expedient for accountability purposes. I proposed it be jointly implemented by the Ministry of Youth and Social Development and DSVRT. The

Executive Order helped to contextualise the issues we were battling with, and then highlight, emphasise and reiterate the state governor's political will in addressing these issues from both a preventive and responsive approach.

After drafting the memorandum communicating this new position, it was signed by Mrs Ibirogba. It was delivered to the Attorney-General for further directives. I kept following up on the memorandum but didn't get any response.

We continued with the task ahead, responding to various forms of Sexual and Gender-Based Violence. Then on one fine day in September 2016, I received a call from the Office of the Vice President of Nigeria in respect of a particular case of defilement, which was alleged to have occurred in a very prominent school. The affected child who was two years plus was able to disclose the abuse to her mother.

At the time the case was being reported to me, the police had already got involved, and the child had already received medical attention which confirmed that indeed, she had been sexually abused.

However, the school appeared to be complacent about the case, and as such, the mother of the child was very apprehensive as to whether she would be able to get justice for her child or not.

After being able to speak with the mother, we advised that both she and her daughter receive psychosocial support, another form of evidence which we believed would corroborate her child's disclosure.

Considering it allegedly occurred in the school, the mother was informed that my office would have to write to the school, and we would visit the school. The purpose of our visit would not be to enquire or investigate the allegation, but to ascertain which child protection policies, if any, were in place, to ensure children can make disclosures and if there were designated Child Protection Officers to receive such disclosures. We also wanted to know if the children are regularly sensitised about their rights, responsibilities, and child abuse. We also wanted to know if there were other affected children, etc.

A formidable delegation comprising members of DSVRT and officials from Office of Education Quality Assurance as well as officers from the School Social Work Department visited the school on 7 December 2016. Upon our interaction with the school management, we found out that though a Child Protection document existed, it was not fully operational. Furthermore, students, particularly Nursery and Primary school students were not regularly informed about their rights, Child Abuse, Maltreatment, Neglect, Sexual and Gender-Based Violence generally.

It was also discovered that teachers and school administrators were not sufficiently trained on Child's Rights and their role as First Responders. A worrisome discovery was the fact that there was no clear-cut protocol on how to address disclosure of abuse.

The content of the Child Protection Policy was not disseminated effectively. In terms of human personnel, it was also discovered that there was no Guidance Counsellor to cater for nursery school pupils. There was also no Social Worker responsible for attending to Nursery and Primary School students.

These findings were altogether very worrisome particularly because of the status of the school that was being investigated. This reminded me of what my good friend and *egbon,* Mr Taiwo Akinlami had told me: 'Schools in Nigeria generally do not value safety and protection, and neither do parents. There is a lot of focus on the curriculum, standard of teaching, the prestige and legacy of the school, but very few people actually find out if the schools they intend to enrol their children in, have a safeguarding and child protection policy in place, so when there is no demand, the supplier is at liberty to offer only the services that are being requested for.'

The level of investment in child protection policies in schools at that time was abysmal.

Nonetheless, we documented our findings and wrote back to the school, highlighting the above lapses and requesting urgent actions to be taken. Unfortunately for the school, but fortunately for us, the media had got wind of the case, and they had provided press coverage of the first time when the suspect was arraigned before the Magistrate Court.

The school, a popular one, had a reputation on the line, with the case having gone viral on blogs and social media. At around 11 p.m., on 4 December 2016, I received an email from my boss, Mr Adeniji Kazeem, SAN, forwarding a brief narration of the case by the child's mother. In my reply the following day, I informed him of the status of the criminal case and also the steps we intended to take, to ensure such allegation never repeats itself.

I ended the email by expressing the challenges we were encountering in ensuring schools, particularly private schools adopt and implement a Safeguarding and Child Protection Policy, bearing in mind that the state was yet to adopt ours. At around 10:55p.m. that same day, he acknowledged receipt of my email, and this time copied the Deputy Governor who was the superintendent of the Ministry of Education, H.E. Mrs Idiat Adebule as well as the Special Adviser of Education, Mr Fela Bank-Olemoh with a view to solicit their support in ensuring the policy was swiftly ratified by the Government. Unfortunately, when this email came in, I was already asleep.

At around 2 a.m. on 6 December 2016, the Governor, Mr Akinwunmi Ambode sent a mail to my boss in which I was copied, requesting us to expedite action on the policy. At around 4 a.m., the Deputy Governor replied to the Governor's email acknowledging his directive. At this time, I was wide awake, buzzing with excitement.

At around 4:48a.m., I summoned courage and replied the Deputy Governor's email, informing Her Excellency that a subcommittee had been constituted, the policy had been drafted, circulated amongst relevant ministries, same had been validated, and now presented in the format of an Executive Order for the Governor's ratification. The relevant documents were attached to the email. I thought it was expedient that this was done, so everyone was aware that all we were waiting for was the Governor's signature. I sent the email and hoped for the best.

At around 5:40a.m., the Deputy Governor replied my boss, informing him that she had received the draft policy, and would ensure we receive her feedback on it that same day.

At around 6:16a.m. I received a phone call, it was the Deputy Governor of Lagos State, informing me that she would expedite action. Also, she gave assurance that the Governor would ratify the policy in the next few days.

As I got off the phone, I started jumping for joy, I was filled with excitement. I rushed to my husband who was awake, and told him everything that had transpired. I was so elated. True to her words, ten days later, on 16 December 2016, I received a call from my boss informing me that the Governor had signed the policy, and that the signed copies would be available for pick up the following day.

I reflected and concluded that this took approximately two weeks to actualise, mainly because there was practical insight into the usefulness of such a policy. The eye-opener for me was the need to pinpoint the value-add of what one's idea or proposal brings to the table, and find a key stakeholder or sponsor who can help drive the political will and see things through.

I learnt that with political will, the impossible would become possible. I also learnt that no force could stop an idea whose time had come. Circumstances would fall in place to ensure that it became a reality.

Since then, as a team, we have engaged over 4,000 officers in Child Protection trainings, multi-agency trainings, comprising educators, health workers, law enforcement personnel, social workers, non-governmental organisations, etc.

In 2019, we partnered with the Teaching Service Commission during the recruitment of over 1000 teachers; to ensure safer recruitment procedures were adhered to and adopted. Immediately they were recruited, the teachers were trained on safeguarding and child protection. I am particularly proud of the fact that their Letter of Engagement provides that they undertake to be bound by the provisions of the Safeguarding and Child Protection policy of the state.

In the words of Mr Hakeem Muri-Okunola, who was the then Permanent Secretary of the Ministry of Youth and Social Development and a key supporter of the DSVRT idea, 'the Safeguarding and Child Protection Policy is like a magic wand'. We have over the years, ensured the full implementation, created awareness, and used it as leverage in ensuring enforcement of the rights of children, their total well-being and their protection.

While modest progress and gains have been made since the 16th of December 2016, there is certainly a lot more ground to cover. Nonetheless, we keep hope alive.

CHAPTER 8

RESPONDING TO DOMESTIC VIOLENCE

Before DSVRT came onto the scene, most of the reported cases of domestic violence were being addressed by mediation, but towards settlement and reconciliation of the parties. Very few cases where the survivors were courageous enough would end up in court, mostly for a restraining order only.

Though I'd want to boast of the work I and my team have been doing, domestic violence remains a sensitive issue. Nobody wants to get involved in a 'husband and wife issue'. Afterall, we were not there when they met each other, they may also reconcile.

Of a truth, when we began DSVRT, most of the attention was on sexual violence. Our fliers, posters, awareness campaigns were mostly on sexual violence. I recall one of those days that Mrs Bose Ironsi drew my attention to it. 'There is need to also give attention to and propose policies targeted at domestic violence,' she said in one of our meetings.

Mrs Ironsi's NGO, Women's Rights and Health Project had done amazing work in Alimosho community, ensuring the domestic violence law was simplified and disseminated in a manner that members of the community could appreciate and relate with. Thus, we started placing greater focus on being deliberate about our response mechanisms on domestic violence.

This led us to creating awareness on what survivors wanted. In the bid to do this, we often put up posters listing the demands of survivors. Even though this seemed a long road to follow, even if we had doubts, my faith drowned those doubts and floated me.

Some of the services and requests survivors made included: their need for the beating to stop, their need for the alleged abuser to be cautioned, their need to be believed, their need to leave quietly with the children and if it's a female survivor, for the alleged abuser to provide maintenance and upkeep of the children, their need for adequate legal representation—to file for custody, judicial separation or outright divorce, that they'd like to file a restraining order, preventing the further perpetration of violence, that they'd want for the alleged abuser to be jailed or *tortured* or both, their need to be empowered both financially and emotionally, so they would be able to leave the abusive relationship, and not return due to financial dependence on the abuser.

Deep down, we knew that this list was not just to create awareness, but it was a warning sign, it was a show of presence—a means of telling the perpetrators of these crimes that we, as an organisation, are with the survivors and would do anything within legal jurisdictions give them justice.

Although this list is not exhaustive, majority of the survivors I have been privileged to meet have wanted one or more of the reliefs listed above. Very few have asked if we have a torturing room, where their alleged abuser can be tortured briefly.

Ascertaining what the survivors want is of utmost importance. As a Gender-Based Violence service provider, you cannot assume you know what a survivor wants. I learnt this the hard way.

I remember sometime in 2014, shortly after our inauguration as a team, a lady came to the office, her left eye was swollen, a smudge of purple coloured the top part of her right eye which was barely open due to a punch she had received from her husband. She was light in complexion, so there were a lot of colourings on her face, tiny clots of blood grew out of her skin like dark mushrooms. Across her arms were tiny cuts, streaked like a zebra. She wore a short sleeve top that bare some parts of her skin.

She informed me that she had put to bed two weeks ago, and upon their return home, she got into an argument with her spouse, and he proceeded to dismantle the baby walker, and used one of the parts on her face and her body. Of course, I was livid, I had recently resumed from maternity leave, so I was very aware of the post-natal pains she would have been experiencing, now further exacerbated by this level of violence.

She said she was experiencing great difficulty seeing in that eye and couldn't look up because of the brightness of the sun. Immediately, I took her to the staff clinic in the secretariat and pleaded with the management that she should be treated as an emergency, even though she was not a government staff.

They were magnanimous to agree, and she was referred to the clinician. He was able to dress the eye, prescribe medication and then made an onward referral to an ophthalmologist in the General hospital closest to her. Upon our return, I did a letter to the closest Family Support Unit, and followed up with a call, informing them that it was a high-risk case and requesting it is treated with urgency.

I also didn't want her to be out of the house for too long because of the two-week-old baby who was left at home with her own mother. She informed me that after the incident, her husband had left the house, so she didn't feel she was in any immediate danger.

Nevertheless, I asked that she visited the hospital and the police station immediately. The next day, the police called and informed me that the husband had been arrested, and he admitted to physically assaulting her. However, the complainant had been begging on his behalf, and had offered to bail him. I said it wasn't possible, that the officer should kindly ask the survivor to come to my office at her earliest convenience.

To my greatest surprise, she came later that day, in the company of her two-year-old daughter, with the infant strapped to her mother's back. She started with the usual prayers in the Yoruba dialect, 'Your home will not break. You have stood for me; the Lord will get up for you. You will not mourn over your children,' she pleaded. At this point, I had become impatient. 'What is going on?' I asked.

It was the devil that made my husband do what he did. His family members have come to beg, the mosque have got involved, and they have pleaded that I drop the case. I think we should leave it to God

She pleaded, leaning towards my table, rubbing her palms in a prayer and a plea. I was livid. I remember asking her if she felt the work I was doing in my office was a joke to her. What she said next would have made me burst into laughter if I wasn't furious at the same time.

'Madam, please just forget I even came,' she replied, continuing in the plea, this time on her knees.

The old mother's knees were about to hit the ground when I got up and asked them to desist from what they were doing. The mother told me that they would make sure either the husband leaves the house, or they would raise funds for her to secure accommodation, but one thing is certain—they were not going to be together. However, they did not want him prosecuted.

'Please, madam, consider the children, who would walk them down the aisle?' the old woman asked.

At this point, I reiterated that the office was particularly concerned about her safety, and if truly they were going to be separated, then perhaps, he should be made to write an undertaking at the police station to desist from perpetrating any further form of violence, and he should commit to either leaving the house for her and the children, or he would secure accommodation for them.

I remember after the lady left, I took some time to think, process, and dissect what had just happened. Here I was, thinking what she wanted was to jail him, but I then recalled that she never said anything about prosecution. I was the one who felt that should be the corresponding action especially given the violence meted out against her. Unfortunately, that did not amount to justice for the survivor. She wanted a separation, a situation where he would continue to provide maintenance and his access to the children and her would be supervised.

This singular event altered my approach to handling domestic violence cases. I became more survivor-centred. Indeed, the survivor is at the heart of the process. But there is a caveat when life is threatened, we ensure safety of the survivor first, and this may even entail placing the survivor in a shelter and proceeding with the criminal case, without the survivor's consent.

I remember that at some point, I was referred to as the 'Breaker of Homes'. We had some alleged abusers who would accuse us of conniving with their spouse, simply because we did not 'beg' or attempt to convince the survivor to go back and return to the alleged abuser.

This, in their view, meant that we were breaking their homes. Some alleged abusers would ask me: 'Are you not married? Why don't you want my wife and I to reconcile?' And my answer to this was always simple.

Every time I go home, I should be able to sleep soundly, not worrying that a client is in distress at home, at risk of being 'Late Mrs' simply because I asked her to return to her place of abuse. Nobody's blood would be on my hands. After all, separation is not divorce. People need to be alive, whole, complete, safe and comfortable before they can work on their relationship.

We also had people refer to us a *women's movement.* Perhaps because at that time, most of the cases being reported were by women. It could also have been because a majority of the Gender Based Violence Cases officers in my office were all female!

Imagine a man, experiencing domestic violence, walks into an office filled with women, there is a high likelihood for him to feel he would not get *justice.* Optics and first impression truly mattered. This made us more deliberate in ensuring we were able to engage at least 30% of male officers, especially mediators who would preside over domestic violence cases in the office.

However, this is an area we are still working on to crack; ensuring we are able to create a safe space for men to speak out. Handling domestic violence needs to be from a kaleidoscope of social, legal, financial, medical and psychosocial perspectives. The idea that once a domestic violence case is reported, the immediate response should be mediation should be jettisoned. Not all cases have to go through mediation, especially when there is evidence of the abuse (which unfortunately isn't always the case in at least 60% of the cases). Government, nongovernmental organisations, law enforcement, and the society generally are mostly disposed to 'helping' them 'settle' their differences. People ostensibly assume the role of peacemaker, and end up making matters even worse for the survivor.

In the absence of the abuser submitting himself/herself for psychosocial support, mediation would not deter an abuser from perpetrating further violence. The idea of families or other formal institutions 'settling' domestic violence would at best, *temporarily* prevent any further form of abuse.

Even at that, the abuse usually then manifests in other forms, such as verbal, emotional, financial, and psychological. This, in my view, worsens the situation as when survivors summon the courage and reach out again, they are told, 'at least he is not beating you. He is paying school fees, taking care of the children, just manage'. They therefore feel trapped, silenced, and coerced into remaining in toxic, abusive relationships, until they can summon enough courage again and speak out.

Without forgetting that no form of violence is graver than the other, the impact of emotional, psychological, and verbal abuse can have a devastating impact on the victim's mental health. It is heart breaking to see a survivors of domestic violence, diagnosed as being clinically depressed, suffering from schizophrenia, attempted suicide or is committed to a psychiatric facility.

Eventually, like the biblical Job, what they feared the most, happens. The children are taken, they lose the marriage and lose the child (ren), lose everything and more often than not, the abuser goes scot free.

I am constrained to remember to be survivor-centred throughout, so in instances where the client/ survivor insists on not wanting to escalate to the police station, most times, we have no choice but to oblige. When I attend to such cases in the office, I deploy more of negotiation than mediation. This is because after clearing the issue of the allegation of domestic violence, we then seek to examine whether or not the parties want to remain together or be separated and this is where the negotiation takes place, especially if there are children involved.

Over the years, I have noticed that in circumstances where the client (female), reports domestic violence, and she is no longer willing to remain in the abusive relationship, the alleged abuser uses the children as a pawn/leverage, weapon. That is where you hear some alleged abuser indicate his desire to provide a meagre sum of five thousand naira (N5,000) monthly for two children, and if that amount is not satisfactory, the children should be returned to him. Meanwhile, he is the one who mentioned that he buys foodstuff in the house and spends on average, twenty thousand naira monthly.

Most times, at this juncture, one has to resort to negotiation. During this whole process, we reiterate the paramount principle, the best interest of the child, and also emphasise that the children are innocent. Unfortunately, this doesn't work many times, simply because, this gesture of determining how much to provide is still part of the desire of an abuser to *control and dominate* their victim. So, what is the solution? *EMPOWERMENT! EMPOWERMENT!! EMPOWERMENT!!!* Everyone, particularly women, need to be empowered. As I say often in the office; *there is nothing as sexy as a woman that is empowered. There is a limit to the abuse she would take from an abusive spouse/partner.*

Does this mean that a financially secure woman is immune from being a victim of domestic violence? No, but women who are empowered would know they have options, they have choices. They can quickly raise funds to secure accommodation, they can quickly pay for school fees and hope it would be reimbursed, they can afford to feed their children. They are not hungry or homeless. So, they can think, plan and decide on the next step to take. Survivors who are financially dependent on their abuser unfortunately may not have that luxury.

Indeed, survivors of domestic and sexual violence may suffer from financial strains as devastating as their physical injuries and emotional trauma. The financial difficulties may emanate from unpaid medical bills, and the inability to work caused by injury, etc. Even more pressing is the fact that financial stress often leaves survivors stuck in abusive relationships because their partners are often the breadwinners of the home, and they do not have any source of income to take care of themselves and their children on their own.

I recall that a particular survivor of domestic violence had got so accustomed to visiting us in the office. Granted, her case was still on going as the alleged abuser had not been apprehended. However, it had become a routine that whenever she is ready to go home, she would request some financial support for transportation and to feed her four-yearold daughter. Members of staff were very conversant with the client's story, so everyone would willingly contribute to the survivor. One fine day, after visiting us in the office, as she was about to leave, I asked her what she could do if she had some financial support.

To my amazement, she responded that she could sell drinks and local gin and she had already made enquiries as to the best places to strategically position her products. I asked her to think about all that she would need to start, and assign the amount for each item. She came up with a list of items that would cost N48,200 only.

I asked her how much she had, she laughed before responding; 'N4,000 ma, which I have managed to save.' I then reached out to my colleagues in the office and solicited support on her behalf.

Fortunately, I didn't need to do much convincing as the client was pleasant and warm, and over time she had become a *friend* of the office. We raised N50,000 that day, and asked her to commit to providing weekly updates of progress made. As the months went by, the client was able to place her child in a school, she was also able to secure accommodation. Of course, with the progress report we received, we were encouraged and inclined to further support her business.

This was a powerful demonstration of the potentials a survivor of domestic violence could achieve with the right financial support. This is one of the reasons why in 2018, I proposed we establish the Lagos State

Domestic and Sexual Violence Trust Fund to provide substantial financial assistance to victims and their families, where applicable. Furthermore, while no amount of money can erase the trauma and grief victims suffer, this aid can be crucial in the aftermath of abuse.

By paying for care that helps restore victims' physical and mental health, also by replacing lost income for victims who cannot work and for families where the breadwinner is an abuser, the trust fund will assist victims in direct ways. High risk survivors of both domestic and sexual violence would be able to access grants for things like medical expenses, counselling, school fees for the families of victims, business seed money, relocation costs, welfare costs including feeding for the period before the business sets off, protective costs and property loss or restoration.

For domestic violence survivors, they could either access funds for accommodation or for their businesses. Some survivors already had viable businesses, but were in need of financial support, others wanted to venture into business but required funds.

For the latter category, we entered into a partnership with SME 100, (a youth-led organisation that inspires, empowers, and equips young entrepreneurs and small and medium scale enterprises), founded by Mr Charles Odii to empower survivors in this regard. Asides from providing grants, we organised an empowerment training programme which was conceived to serve as a pathway to new beginnings for survivors and also rebuild their self-esteem.

Over a period of one month, participants were taken on different modules around the theme 'Passion to Profit'. The modules included courses like Accessing my Passion, Developing a Vision, Matching my Skills with Visions, Goals setting, Achieving your goals, Business and Professional Ethics, Assessing Demand and Market size, Estimating cost, Customer Segmentation and Effective Communication. They were also trained on Financial Resources: Sources of Capital, Money Management, Business Planning, Business Model canvass, and Value Creation.

Participants that needed employment were also trained. They were taken on the various topics like Navigating the Job Market, Employability skills, Problem solving, critical and creative thinking, Communication Skills, Emotional Intelligence, Teamwork, Effective Presentation Skills, Personal Communication and Intrapreneurship. They were also trained on Writing an effective CV/Resume and How to Successfully Navigate Job Interviews.

At the end of the training, participants were given an opportunity to pitch their ideas to leading stakeholders in their respective industries. Most importantly, participants were assigned to mentors and given internship opportunities in order to further harness their skills and gain practical experience.

Through this Trust Fund, DSVRT was able to financially empower over 60 women to establish their businesses, strengthened existing businesses or require assistance in relocation. I have also learned that most survivors in this category need continuous support, hand-holding and mentorship if they are to succeed and attain financial independence.

The unfortunate reality is that some would not be successful because of the various challenges they encounter.

These challenges most often stem from the need to be sole providers for the children since their abuser has refused to provide, or adequately provide for the children, so they resort to making use of their profit. Consequently, they are unable to reinvest back into the business. Unfortunately, we also had few survivors who returned to the abuser after receiving the training and the grants. I am not yet certain if this can be avoided in its entirety.

Also, some are not business-minded. Some survivors thrive better when gainfully employed, so for the empowerment programme to be successful, there is a need for qualified survivors to be able to access job placements.

On my own part, through the Lola Vivour-Adeniyi Foundation also referred to as Merchant of Hope, I have had the opportunity of financially supporting over 35 survivors of domestic violence and their children's education and registering a business. This has brought me fulfilment. In truth, these days I sleep at night with the satisfaction that I have, through Merchant of Hope foundation, been able to empower survivors and guide them out of abuse and abusive relationships.

Empowering survivors is extremely critical to providing holistic support to survivors.

Govenor Akinwunmi Ambode meeting with members of the Lagos State Domestic and Sexual Violence Response Team on 30 September 2017 in commemoration of the Domestic and Sexual Violence Awareness Month.

Handing over of Rape Kits to the Primary Health Care Board on 1 June 2016.

Presentation of cheque from Northwest Petroleum Limited to the Permanent Secretary, Primary Health care Board, Dr Sodeinde on 1 June 2016.

Launch of Sexual Intervention Trust Fund to cater to medical support for survivors of Sexual Violence in State health facilities in Lagos State on 10 December 2020

Governor Babatunde Raji Fashola, SAN signing the executive order establishing the Sex Offenders Register and Mandated Reporting Programme on 1 December 2014.

Governor Akinwunmi Ambode, flanked by Hon. Chief Judge of Lagos State, Hon. Justice Oke as well as the representative of the Rt. Hon. Speaker of the Lagos State House of Assembly, Hon. Abiru as well as other top government functionaries during the symbolic Walk against Sexual and Gender-Based Violence on 13 March 2018.

Engagement of Obas in Council on 11 May 2016.

Symbolic Walk to Commit and Act, led by Governor Sanwo-Olu on 26 November 2019, in commemoration of 16 Days of Activism

Governor Sanwo-Olu signing into Law the Domestic and Sexual Violence Agency Bill, 2021 on 20 September 2021.

Governor Sanwo-Olu signing the Commitment to act Statement on 26 November 2019.

Launch of the Lagos State Sexual Assault Standing Order, the first of its kind in Nigeria, as well as the Sexual Assault Evidence Collection Kits, also referred to as Rape Kits on 26 February 2016.

WALK TO COMMIT AND ACT: RESTATING LAGOS STATE GOVERNMENT'S ZERO TOLERANCE STANCE ON SEXUAL AND GENDER-BASED VIOLENCE

COMMITMENT STATEMENT

PREAMBLE

Guided by the vision, aspirations and hopes of the founding fathers of Lagos State, which are underpinned by justice and progress for all and recalling that all residents of Lagos State (regardless of gender, creed or economic status) have certain universal, indivisible and inalienable human rights:

1. We acknowledge that all residents of Lagos State, including women and girls, have the right to thrive and harness their full potentials without the fear or threat of any form of sexual and gender-based violence;

2. The incidences of rape, sexual assault, domestic abuse and child abuse among other forms of sexual and gender-based violence perpetuated across Lagos State are appalling;

3. Being the Executive Arm of Government, we are aware of our role in maintaining a Zero Tolerance stance on sexual and gender-based violence towards creating a safer and more prosperous Lagos State for all;

4. We are convinced that the total commitment of the Lagos State Government is critical for transforming social norms that, enable sexual and gender-based violence, perpetuate inequality and clog the wheel of justice.

I, BABAJIDE O. SANWO-OLU hereby restate my commitment to the eradication of sexual and domestic violence in Lagos State. As an integral part of the Lagos State Executive Council, I commit to using the powers and privileges of my office as GOVERNOR OF LAGOS STATE (within the ambit of the law) to end sexual and gender-based violence within the State. I further commit to actively collaborate with and support all relevant agencies towards engaging in strategic policy advocacy, sustaining preventive interventions, providing medical and psycho-social support and seeking justice for the survivors of sexual and gender-based violence.

This I pledge solemnly and freely on this **26th day of November 2019** at LAGOS

(Name and Signature of Committer)

T. J. [illegible]
(Name and Signature of DSVRT Representative)

Babajide Olusola Sanwo-Olu
Governor of Lagos State
Lagos House, Secretariat, Alausa, Ikeja, Lagos. Tel: 09017077777
E-mail: bosgov@lagosstate.gov.ng

CHAPTER 9

THE MEDIA/PARTNERSHIPS/VISIBILITY INNOVATIONS

The days swooped past us like migratory birds, screeching, as we ramped up the battle for the safety of our women and children. Time and time again, I sauntered into the worlds of my imagination, drifting on utopian cloud flakes, away from the sufferings of the world. I would catch myself and a smile will smear my face. I would remind myself that I needed to be here and now. Sometimes, I fixed my mind on any external stimuli I could find, perhaps a spinning fan or even the sound of my breathing, and held it that way for some time, calling back my thought whenever it strayed. It was a form of meditation for me, to prepare my mind for the dizzying pace of the coming months.

When the team became fully operational, and I started handling cases in my office in 2015, it was clear that we had to have a toll-free line, to encourage people to report. Since we did not have funds to secure a toll-free line, we partnered with the Lagos State Emergency Management Agency (LASEMA), the agency in charge of the Lagos State's emergency help line – 767/112.

This was a pertinent move. One of the key elements of our work was the removal of barriers to the obtainment of healthcare provisions and justice, then it was necessary to consider how financial impediments might negatively affect the instance of reportage at any given time. I was trying to put myself in the shoes of women who, for whatever reasons, might not have the means to communicate with us as when they needed to. And that, I could see, was a unique kind of hell in itself. Pulling down the financial barrier to the best of our abilities was, therefore, utterly necessary.

We trained the Command Control Centre operatives on receiving calls on domestic violence and sexual violence. As first responders, they need to communicate empathy, belief and also encourage survivors on what to do and where to go. This necessitated us drawing up a call centre tool kit, not knowing it would become instrumental for our own call centre which was launched almost five years later.

After each of these programmes, be it the training of operatives of the Command Control Centre, engagement of the Iya Loja General of Nigeria, Iya Lojas and Baba Lojas of Lagos, or the engagement of the Oba of Lagos, and Obas in council, I would do a press release, and share with the then Chief Press Secretary, Mr. Habib Aruna. I worked very closely with Mr Ekene Okoro in the CPS's office who assisted in ensuring that the releases were sent out, particularly in time for Monday morning.

Social media also played a key role in pushing our stories far and wide, and we received organic support from so many people who out of genuine concern saw it fit to re-share any message we posted. I remember setting up the DSVRT Twitter account at a time I had barely operated my own personal account—I would not consider myself as being social media savvy—however, looking back in time, setting up a Twitter account was pivotal in building our image. Also, what better way could there be to connect with today's youths than to maintain an active social media presence? I am continually appreciative of all those who helped us spread the word and still do to this day without any sort of prompting. Individuals like Mrs Juliet Kego Ume-Onyido, Mr Akin Oyebode, Mr Jubril Gawat, Dr Joe Abah, Mr Babafemi Oretuyi, Ms Karo Omu and others too numerous to mention have been very supportive of the cause, and have used their social media platforms to amplify our messages.

In my opinion, I believe what helped significantly grow our prominence were the various press releases we were pushing out, our growing social media presence, openly sharing our data trends, as well as the diverse cases we were handling.

Despite not having resources, I was determined to make sure we got so big that we could no longer be ignored. This was light we were hoping to bring to the people who had been thrust into darkness. Surely, no one lights a lamp and hides it under a bushel, but on the table top to illuminate the surrounding. Our light was radiating in fluorescent rapidity. The heavens noticed, so did the state. Governor Ambode was in love with our cause, and was committed to funding our proposed activities. On this basis, we were able to achieve the following only one year into Governor Ambode's Administration: The designation of the month of September as Domestic and Sexual Violence Awareness Month—this was to coincide with the month the team was inaugurated, 11 September 2014.

The month would begin with a media parley with Lagos State Government Office correspondents. It was an opportunity to discuss data, trends observed, activities embarked on, notable cases, gains made, prosecutions, etc. It was a pleasurable two hours because we would be speaking with press correspondents who are conversant with the issues, so the conversations were intelligent and enlightening. We would then select a day in the next week after the media parley where we would have road walks, community outreaches. This was another opportunity to ensure that residents of Lagos State were abreast of the issues and informed of who to reach out to access help.

A symposium would follow. Rich and deep conversations about the issues, and we were always blessed with distinguished resource persons. Usually, we would have a communiqué, which would be circulated amongst relevant policy makers and stakeholders for implementation. Indeed, it was at one of the symposiums where it was suggested that the DSVRT begin to pay stronger attention to the male folk. This was particularly significant, bearing in mind that statistics had shown that even though men are more likely to perpetrate abuse, boys are also vulnerable to experiencing abuse.

It was therefore expedient that boys were engaged at an early age on promoting positive masculinity, dismantling patriarchy, changing the attitude and behavioural mindset of boys as it relates to their perception of Sexual and Gender-Based Violence, the need to act as protectors rather than perpetrators, also, the knowledge and tools to assist in the prevention of Gender-Based Violence. These were some of the reasons for the Kings Club Initiative for boys.

A day would be selected in the 4th week of September for our Commendation night, a sparkling event of glee, bright lights and glamour. This was the climax and highlight for me and others. Apart from the flamboyance, I also felt it was extremely important that people working in this field are celebrated. Police officers, social workers, counsellors, health workers, non-governmental organisations, practitioners, service providers and the media who go beyond the call of duty daily while responding to incidents of Sexual and Gender-Based Violence. It was therefore only appropriate that they are celebrated, recognised and honoured at least once a year in grand style.

These moments we designed not only to signify our collective break from stress, but also our collective celebration of our little victories and reaffirmation of our hope and desire to continue on the path of truth and service for the greater good.

As responders, we are also exposed to secondary trauma. And so, dedicating a day in the year to unwind was both necessary and therapeutic, in my opinion. And this opinion, obviously, was shared by many other people too. By investing ourselves in stories replete with dark themes, we exposed ourselves to mental stress in exceptional ways. Themes that seeped into our subconscious and punished us, sometimes in ways we couldn't properly express. We saw unwinding to be more than mere luxury. It was a necessity. Also, it was an opportunity to showcase our achievements and outline the proposed activities we were hoping to implement in the coming year.

With each year, we tried to make it more glamorous, better than the previous year and a night to remember. Indeed, the awards night was the icing on the cake, an event that members looked forward to. We designed six categories of awards: best Health facility, Best Social Welfare office, Mandated Reporter, Best NGO, Best Family Support Unit, and Special Award Category.

We also made use of the Commendation night to publicly acknowledge the support of corporate organisations like MTN, Access Bank, Airtel, Northwest Petroleum Plc, Unilever, UAC Foods, Fan Milk, etc. who had supported us in one way or the other. This, we believed, was necessary for encouraging and fostering partnerships with the private sector. Over the years, the overall feedback we received from guests that attended the Commendation Dinner was always very encouraging. Participants were always very appreciative of the opportunity to unwind, socialise and be celebrated. For me, taking time away from thinking about deep issues proved to be refreshing and renewing. After savouring wines and other drinks, munching on delicacies, and having my beauty sleep, I felt ready to take on the world again. New ideas would flood me and the team upon resumption of duty.

Another innovation was the securing of a USSD Short code for reporting cases of Domestic and Sexual Violence as well as Child Abuse. This was achieved in 2018 after Governor Ambode gave the approval and the funds for this. We chose the USSD instead of a mobile application for reporting because some of our survivors may not own smart phones. So long as they could send and receive text messages on their phone, they would access support. This was also at a time where it had become unequivocally clear that we had to leverage technology in our war against Sexual and Gender-Based Violence.

The idea for the USSD short code was birthed in 2017 when I was invited to attend and deliver special remarks at the Rule of Law in Sub-Saharan Africa Symposium organised by the Rule of Law Collaborative under the auspices of the Justice Sector Training, Research and Coordination Program in Cape Town, South Africa. This invitation was facilitated by Mr Olufunmbi Falayi of The Hague Institute for Innovation of Law (HiiL).

A fellow participant spoke about what his organisation was doing in Malawi to ensure people in the rural areas were able to access maternal healthcare support through a USSD short code and SMS. I was so impressed and inspired. I had an epiphany at that moment as the participant's words funnelled through my pinna. Light bulbs in my brain were lit, as though a strange and rampant current had passed through them instantaneously. My brain began to work animatedly on the idea. I plumbed its pros and cons, its utility in the face of our current challenges regarding reportage. The only downside I remember unearthing at the time was that users were charged for every message they sent and automatically received.

I remember returning to Lagos, Nigeria, and beginning do my research on how the USSD short code would work, what was required, and how people would be receptive to it. Taking into cognizance that a significant number of the clients we had been attending to were indigent, we needed to ensure whatever technology we hoped to provide would be at no cost to them. This would also cater to non-internet enabled users.

As God would have it, around that time, NOK 360 reached out, and said they desired to create a mobile application to facilitate reporting of cases. NOK 360 Global Limited is a Value-Added Service company, licensed by Nigerian Communications Commission to provide mobile content and billing services using Short Message Service (SMS), Unstructured Supplementary Service Data (USSD) and Interactive Voice Response (IVR) bearers.

Given our desire to leverage technology, we entered into conversations with management of NOK 360 which comprised of Mr Olalekan Ogunwale, Mrs Omoze LekeApapa, Ms Fope Akinmola, Mr Seyi Eluwole, Emmanuel Oluwatosin, and Arinola Giwa. NOK 360 proposed a threepronged proposition, firstly, to develop a mobile application to facilitate reporting of cases, make use of USSD short code, and deploy Interactive Voice Response (IVR). Instead of commencing with the mobile application, we went for the securing of a USSD short code.

This, we thought, would better serve our demography. As far as the individuals have a telephone, they would be able to reach out to us, and get help. NOK360 helped us secure the USSD short code—*6820* from Nigerian Communications Commission.

Simply by dialling *6820# or sending an SMS to 6820 with a keyword *e.g. child abuse*, users will be fed information on steps to take for the respective case (rape, child abuse, domestic violence). A report would also be logged and forwarded to the appropriate law enforcement, agency or Ministry.

Furthermore, upon sending an SMS to *6820* or dialling **6820#*, users would be taken to an interactive menu browser from which relevant information from such users such as name, location, specific case or complaint would be taken which would in turn ensure that the whole Response Team is automatically stimulated.

Upon dialling or sending a text to 6820, the interface also texts back practical information like details of the closest health facility or police station, and tips on preserving evidence.

With over ten keywords that are translated to Yoruba, English, Pidgin, Igbo and Hausa, this technology solution is home-grown and encourages all residents of Lagos State that have access to a mobile phone to make use of this service.

The major aim of this innovation is to ensure that survivors of all forms of abuse would be able to reach out to the appropriate agencies to receive timely information about what to do, where to go to, how to preserve evidence and most importantly, know how to receive succour. Activation of the short code assists users to identify the nearest legal aid, police stations, healthcare centres, family support units or responsive units whenever a case arises (with the aid of mapping, geotags etc). There would also be a back-end dashboard that interprets inputs received via SMS and profile on the web portal dashboard for all response units to access in real time.

Aside from the immediate response, this technology solution would provide victims with activating *6820* would also assist the State Government in gathering and collating incident information, generating heat-maps within the metropolis, providing automated daily & monthly reporting, providing comprehensive central database/information system and analytics, and providing central information that could also be used for the formulation of prevalence and prevention policies for Lagos State. All of these would be facilitated by NOK 360. The management of NOK 360 was informed that we wanted the users to be able to access this service at no cost.

The suggestion that the telecommunications could provide SMS/USSD at zero cost was then made and that informed our method of engagement with the telecom providers.

Fortunately for us, two of the major telecom providers in Nigeria, Airtel and MTN deemed this initiative worthy and agreed to support it at no cost. We launched the USSD Short code on the 30th of September 2018 at our Commendation Dinner. In the first six months after the launch, we received 1,050 cases via the USSD and SMS platforms.

With this platform, we now have a centralised database for both walk-in clients and cases reported directly through the USSD and SMS platform.

CHAPTER 10

DATA-EVIDENCE BASED POLICY

'In God we trust. All others must bring data.'

This quote, attributed to W. Edwards Deming, was originally meant to emphasise the centrality of data measurement and analysis in the areas of business. However, data gathering and analysis transcends the scope of business, or the rigorous confines of natural sciences. For functional strategies to be created and meaningful inferences that proffer solutions be made, there needs to be a solid, objective basis on which the entire endeavour must rest. This basis would be *data*, collected and stored over periods of time and put under rigorous lens for the ascertainment of truth.

Indeed, during the inception of DSVRT, it became instantly clear that for us to propose policies, design programmes or request funds, we had to have the data. This data would be our fodder, feeding and expanding our knowledge pool, guiding us like a client directs the hands of the masseuse to specific points in the body during massage. Although our data would need to go through a myriad of sessions of analysis, it'd be the primary driving force for our policy formulations as well as programmes we wanted to embark on.

When we commenced operations, we leveraged data from Cleen Foundation. Cleen commissioned a National Crime and Safety Survey in 2012. According to them, the aim of the survey was to obtain information regarding Nigerians' views on the extent, trend and patterns of criminal victimisation in the country. Opinions had been sampled across the country to ascertain amongst other things, the perception people had, incidents where these issues were most prevalent, and the factors responsible for low reportage of Sexual and Gender-Based Violence incidents across the State. Similarly, the research provided disaggregated data of persons affected, most vulnerable and their age brackets.

That data highlighted the fact that at least 80% of citizens sampled expressed their lack of faith and high levels of distrust in the police. This fact was, sadly, to be expected, given the unsavoury reputation of the police in the country. Victims often complained of wondering whether lodging a complaint with the police had any sort of utility whatsoever. Would they take you seriously? Would they seize the opportunity to demand money and exacerbate one's trauma? Would they dismiss it as just another dispensable act of nature? Not worthy of extra attention or effort, time or resources?

This obviously was, and continues to remain a big problem in ensuring survivors can access justice as the police, most times, serve as first responders. The findings of the survey indicated that majority of the residents sampled opined that the mode of dressing, provocative dressing was the major reason why women got raped. However, it is important to state at this point that this opinion is widely contested amongst both lay people and members of the intelligentsia alike. The philosophy that rebuts this assertion comes from two angles:

- The first is that there are too many instances of rape in which the victims were fully clad in socially responsible clothes. Everyone from children to *hijabis* to nuns covered in veils and habits to people dressed in all sorts of professional garbs have been victims of sexual abuse. In no way has it been proven that rape cases have any significant correlation with mode of dressing, however, intuitively, probable that may seem to some people.

- The second opines that the actions of the victim, however provocative or sexually inciteful, does not justify or warrant the perpetuation of the crime. It does not matter if I bathed you with invectives in our strained social encounter, if your response to my actions, however reprehensible they may be, is to pull out a knife and stab me to death.

And one now may say, is raping a person comparable to coldly murdering a person? And the appropriate response is *no one can tell.* However, what we can surely tell is the well documented fact that victims of abuse suffer immensely, sometimes throughout their lifetime. Memories of their trauma lingers on their skin, as they constantly relive their pain in their bodies; it interferes in their work, in proper self-actualisation, in having and maintaining long-term relationships, particularly where it involves sexual intimacy.

It is also not uncommon for abused victims to develop all sorts of mental and personality disorders, or undergo drastic personality changes, often for the worse. Towards the darker ends of the spectrum, self-harm emerges as alternative routes to escape the daunting reality of trauma. In some cases, suicidal thoughts emerge that may lead to suicide. Recently, attention has been drawn to the possibilities of generational abuse, or traducing untreated trauma across generations of people. The reality of abuse, however one looks at it, is harrowing.

Another suggested contributing factor for rape was the lack of self-control by men followed by influence of hard drugs and alcohol. Substance abusers are easily prone to indiscipline of all kinds. The guard rails of societal mores fall apart drastically and crime is perpetuated.

The survey also revealed that over 70% of people sampled disclosed that they would not report a rape case to the police for several reasons, including lack of money to give the police, the inability of the police to apprehend the abuser, fear of disrespect by the police, police asking embarrassing questions, fear of being stigmatised or ostracised, fear that the police may not take the case seriously, etc.

This data, in addition to the mandate given to the DSVRT to influence positive change and ensure efficiency was very critical as we had scientific proofs to support our programmes tailored towards improving the capacity of the police in responding and prosecuting Sexual and Gender Based Violence crimes in the state.

In 2016, when the team was ready to upgrade additional Divisions of the Police to the status of Family Support Units in the State to complement the existing 3 FSUs at the time, we leveraged the data that was available.

The data revealed that certain local governments had a higher prevalence of these incidents. The team was recording high reporting from local governments like Alimosho, Ikorodu, Kosofe, Ifako Ijaiye, Amuwo-Odofin, Ikeja, etc. The data generated between 2015 and 2016 informed the selection of the Divisions to be upgraded. It made it easy to justify our selections as the data was our driving force.

Asides from Local Government Areas with high prevalence, we also focused on areas we weren't receiving cases from. We assumed that perhaps, it was because of the distance to the office that people were not encouraged to report. Conversely, police divisions in local government areas like Badagry and Ajah were included in the upgrade.

That same year, 2016, the team was desirous of preventing sexual violence and to do this, I thought it was expedient to understand why abusers abuse. I was interested in unravelling the tactics commonly used by sex offenders through profiling. Gratefully, the team agreed that this was the right way to proceed, so a team led by a criminologist, (Adetayo Oshinowo), clinical psychologist (Olive Ogedegbe) and a social worker (Kenneth Umunna) was constituted to interview sex convicts in all the prisons (now referred to as correctional facilities).

Other objectives of the study included our desire to make available these variations to members of the public who are most vulnerable to Sexual and Gender-Based Violence, increase the pool of psychologically and mentally knowledgeable people who for some reasons were unaware of these vices and also discover the geographical areas with high rates of sexual violence against women and children.

A total of 131 sex convicts were sampled using both qualitative and quantitative approaches and our findings were truly remarkable. Quite a lot of myths were debunked.

It was discovered that 89% of inmates sampled said they were always under the influence of alcohol, while 10% disclosed that they also abused hard drugs. 69% of the inmates had attained secondary education while 19% had at least primary education.

Most of the inmates were school dropouts, and they confirmed at no point were they informed or taught about Sexual and Gender Based Violence. They further disclosed while they were aware that sexual abuse was an offence, they however equated it with petty stealing or fighting.

80% of the inmates were involved in direct or indirect labour, which therefore showed that most of these perpetrators were employed. This was obviously contrary to the general notion that abusers are idle people, and that is because of their idleness that they commit such heinous acts. We now believe this myth is formulated for convenience purposes; it is easier to dismiss the crime as an unsavoury child of mere idleness than to face the reality that gainfully employed individuals, whose minds are not *the devil's workshops*, are likely agents in the culture of rape.

The game changer for me personally was the discovery that 80.9% of the inmates were abused as children implying that they had become sexually active at an early age. This illustrated the 'abused abuser' paradigm; how abuse often bleeds from one generation into the next. The 'hurt people hurt people' maxim extends here quite evidently. Furthermore, some inmates revealed that they lost their virginity to family members and older acquaintances who took advantage of them during their early teenage years. Painfully, stories like these are often overlooked in the discourse: the sexual predation from some members of the family that often occurs early in the victim's life, which inevitably distorts the victim's perception on interpersonal relationships—particularly with regards to consent and healthy sexual relationships.

Certain factors attributable to reasons given by some inmates who avoid a healthy sex life with their fellow adult include: low self-esteem, impotency and poor sexual performance. This was a common denominator for paedophiles. The data also revealed the top four local governments which were Kosofe, Oshodi, Alimosho and Mushin.

Whilst the study was not successful in ascertaining exact tactics used by perpetrators (i.e., ten rapists could rape for ten different reasons, using different tactics depending on the situation they found themselves in), we however found out that four major underlying factors were recurring decimals in inmates that were sampled which included a history of sexual abuse, low self-esteem of perpetrators, psychological factors and low level of education.

The study made the following recommendations:

1. Treatment programmes should be designed for sex convicts and made open to members of the public suffering from unhealthy sexual addiction to prevent future occurrence or attacks. If utmost

confidentiality is assured, people suffering from unhealthy sexual addiction will be more disposed to come forward for treatment.

2. The Criminal Law of Lagos State 2011, should be amended to provide that anyone found guilty of Rape, Defilement or Sexual Assault by Penetration should serve a minimum of 21 years. This would serve as a deterrence for would be offenders.

3. There is a need to amend the Criminal Law of Lagos State or the Child's Rights Law to provide for 'criminal neglect' which would sanction parents, guardians or care givers who but for their negligence, a child would not have been abused. This, we believed, would serve as a strong deterrence.

4. In view of the fact that certain victims may not be aware that they have been abused, there was a need to educate the public especially young children on Environmental/ Emotional signs to look out for to reduce their chances of being sexually abused. *This type of education may be carried out by including Sex Education in schools' curriculum*, and direct contact i.e., door-to-door campaigns within carefully selected areas especially areas that are densely populated.

5. The images of convicted perpetrators should be shown to the public.

6. Male anti-rape groups should be encouraged in the communities, especially on college campuses. This would encourage other males to take responsibility and not see the cause as a 'female' issue.

Finally, the data revealed that *none of the inmates sampled said mode of dressing was the reason why they sexually assaulted their victim.* This further debunked the myth of the mode of dressing being the reason why perpetrators commit rape. The findings from the data served as a blueprint for programming, and proposition of policies. We could now be strategic in our engagements and advocacy.

This led to our promoting positive masculinity movement, to inspire and engage men as flag bearers in the fight against Sexual and Gender-Based Violence. Given revelations from the study, we started to insist that boys should be invited to attend our flagship education programmes for children and also encourage their active participation. Hitherto, the most emphasis had been placed on the girls.

We were aiming to challenge the culture inside of which the boy child is garbled into an ogre, the culture that hardens him and makes calluses of his heart. For we believe the boy child is a flower, a bloom of possibility, like all children are. But children are impressionable, and perhaps especially so in a social context. They will, more likely than not, manifest the values that are inculcated into them, both expressly and implicitly in the course of their becoming.

Furthermore, the Kings Club initiative was also birthed because of our findings. Leveraging the potency of the educational system in shaping gender perspectives of boys and young men, the Kings Club Initiative essentially seeks to create a sustainable social structure in secondary schools that would help debunk socio-cultural misconceptions, promote positive masculinity and bring about behavioural and attitudinal change in the minds of young boys in Lagos State. The project constitutes an alliance of trained young boys in schools to serve as peer educators and advocates of positive masculinity.

This initiative had been instrumental in the change of behaviours. I once had a conversation with one of the counsellors in Education District VI regarding the impact of this initiative.

'How would you assess the impact of our programme in the short time we've been here?' I asked on a cloudy afternoon, as swallows flapped across the western sky with a light wind stirring the grasses.

'I'd say it's been really helpful... and I say that from personal experience.'

'How do you mean?' I asked, hoping for something specific.

'I know it has just been six weeks of engagement, but I have already seen changes in my boys. Even the way they walk, and their sense of responsibility and commitment to their education. I'm very hopeful.'

This conversation was deeply inspiring to me. Because it was, and still is, absolutely important to me that people of all genders are personally invested in the prevention of abuse, in making the world gentler and less threatening for women.

In a bid to be the repository of data on Sexual and Gender-Based Violence in the state, the team made a proposal to embark on a 2-month community awareness programme. This was from August-September 2016. This was conducted by trained social workers from the University of Lagos. This team was headed by Adetayo Oshinowo, a volunteer par excellence.

The essence of the community awareness outreach was to target inner communities with our gospel of zero tolerance to all forms of Sexual and Gender-Based Violence in the state. We accomplished this through the distribution of relevant informative materials in the form of fliers, posters, stickers, etc. A total of eleven Local Government Areas were visited which included Epe, Ikorodu, Kosofe, Eti Osa, Lagos Mainland, Apapa, Oshodi, Lagos Island, Ojo, Alimosho, and Agege.

Findings revealed that reactions differed across the local governments. Most local government areas we visited were very receptive to the field officers, whilst some other local government areas were rather hostile. Some residents believed this (creating awareness about Domestic and Sexual Violence), was not what government was supposed to concern itself with. There were far more pressing challenges i.e., unemployment, lack of power, lack of access to clean water, etc. that required urgent government action. And while one can understand the residents' frustration with the political apathy of the ruling class across the country (to which I dare say Lagos State continues to strive to make the lives of all residents more conducive by the day), one can also not help but notice how the subject of abuse had essentially become opportunity cost in the scale of preference of those communities. The urgency of tackling its evil had been relegated to lower-order priority, as though the instance of perceived governmental neglect somehow made the harrowing realities of abuse victims less valid and less real.

We also used this opportunity to administer a survey to measure the perception of Lagosians towards Sexual and Gender-Based Violence, level of knowledge about the relevant laws. A majority of the residents sampled advocated for tougher punishment—people wanted convicted rapists to be castrated, the punishment should be a death penalty instead of life imprisonment and they also wanted accelerated hearing of the cases in court.

Some residents sampled proffered recommendations they felt would be critical in winning the war against Sexual and Gender-Based Violence, some of which included the establishment of DSVRT clubs in primary and secondary schools, and establishing district offices across the state. Some respondents also suggested that the state should create specialised Sexual and Gender-Based Violence law enforcement officers that would carry out supportive investigation, to complement the efforts of the police. They felt that this would go a long way in increasing offender responsibility and restoring public confidence and trust in the system.

The team conducted another community engagement in 2017. This time it was over a period of six months, between July and December 2017. This time around, we were able to secure more funding from the State

Government and so we increased our coverage. We were able to go to all the local government areas but with special focus in these areas; Agege, Ajeromi-Ifelodun, Alimosho, Amuwo-Odofin, Apapa, Badagry, Epe, Eti-Osa, Ibeju-Lekki, Ifako-Ijaiye, Ikeja, Ikorodu, Kosofe, Lagos Island, Lagos Mainland, Mushin, Ojo, Oshodi-Isolo, Shomolu, and Surulere.

As a team, we took the advocacy to schools, religious institutions, markets, health facilities, financial institutions and more exciting, door-to-door community engagement. They took it into the sun and into the wind, harnessing the elements to spread the message. I remember seeing a picture of researchers in a home, preaching the Zero Tolerance message to the father, mother and their three children. My heart glowed, and I was filled with hope.

It is instructive to note that the selection of places to visit was strategic. Markets, being what they are, are not just places for commerce but also places where information can spread easily because individuals [from all walks of life] with different backgrounds and experiences get to converge within the (market) space from time to time. It is noteworthy to emphasise that the markets were fruitful grounds for the actualisation of the campaign's goals as the team was also able to make people know that they were never the REASONS for these abuses.

The data also showed a low level of awareness about relevant laws that ensured the protection of survivors and also an increase in offender responsibility and accountability. Residents that we were privileged to engage about the Protection Against Domestic Violence Law, 2015, found it unbelievable and ludicrous that a domestic violence abuser could be restrained from coming to his house, if a Restraining/ Protection Order is successfully granted by the court against them.

Some said this was completely ridiculous and that government should respect the sanctity of marriage, a union ordained by God himself.

Once, a displeased individual howled at us: *'This is not America or Europe. Lagos is not London. We have a culture here!'*

And I shook my head in utter dismay. Sometimes, it isn't easy navigating the shocking oppositions we encounter on the field. The people who say these measures are egregious say so as though our culture is more tolerable of violence and disrespect for one another. As if development was alien to our very fabric. As if Nigerian women and *'suffer head'* were one and the same.

In the spirit of looking at the cup half full, I decided to see this as a learning experience. Indeed, it is not enough to enact a law or formulate a policy that is expected to have a direct impact on the citizenry without embarking on pre and post-public consultations. If this Domestic Violence Law would be instrumental in protecting survivors of Domestic Violence, then the people need to know about its existence.

Furthermore, the data revealed that there was still a low level of awareness about what amounts to Sexual and Gender-Based Violence, especially Domestic Violence. Interestingly, the data revealed that people in Badagry were the most knowledgeable about what Sexual and GenderBased Violence as well as child abuse entailed.

All our findings from the various engagements were instrumental in subsequently designing advocacy programmes, information education and communication materials to facilitate information sharing, and grass-root community engagements which we believed were critical in changing mindsets.

One of the major objectives for these community engagements was essentially to create awareness about Sexual and Gender-Based Violence, encourage the culture of mandatory reporting, and increase awareness about the existence of DSVRT. We believed all of these, put together, would in turn increase the number of reported cases. The below infographic reveals just how successful we were at this.

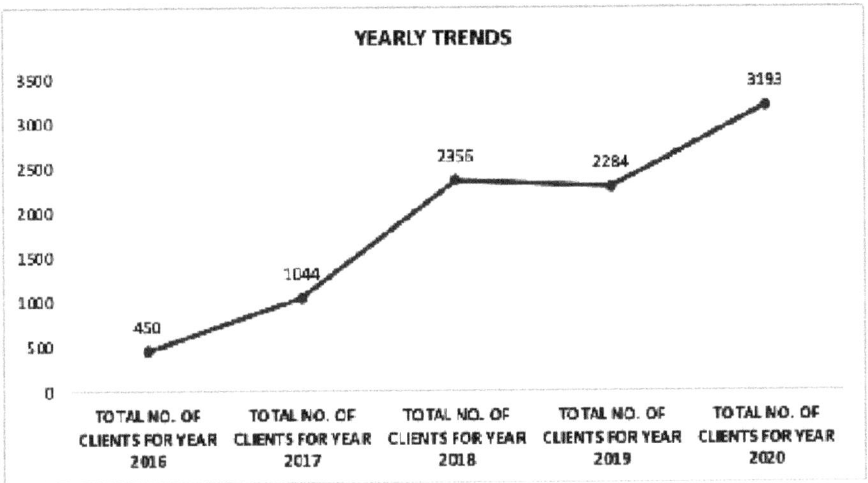

Worthy of note is the fact that we did not embark on any community engagement after 2017. Therefore, we were benefitting from the cumulative aftermath of the community engagements.

Conversely, in our desire to become the repository of Sexual and Gender-Based Violence data in the State, I supervised the analysis of data from domestic violence cases received in the office, between 2015 till 2017. The objective was to unravel any common denominator in cases and our findings summarised in the infographic below were quite instructive.

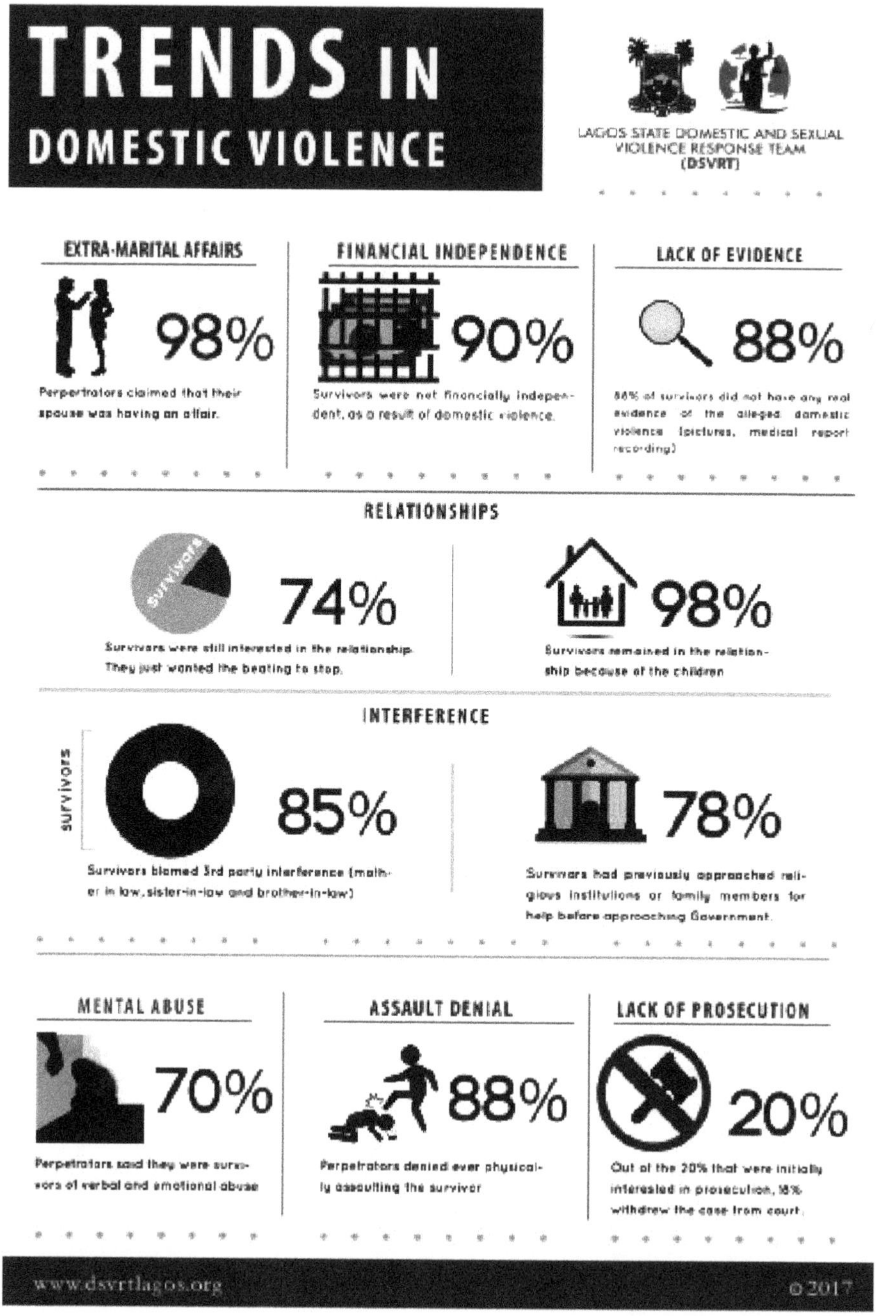
TRENDS IN DOMESTIC VIOLENCE
LAGOS STATE DOMESTIC AND SEXUAL VIOLENCE RESPONSE TEAM (DSVRT)
EXTRA-MARITAL AFFAIRS
98%
Perpetrators claimed that their spouse was having an affair.
FINANCIAL INDEPENDENCE
90%
Survivors were not financially independent, as a result of domestic violence.
LACK OF EVIDENCE
88%
88% of survivors did not have any real evidence of the alleged domestic violence (pictures, medical report recording)
RELATIONSHIPS
survivors
74%
Survivors were still interested in the relationship. They just wanted the beating to stop.
98%
Survivors remained in the relationship because of the children
INTERFERENCE
survivors
85%
Survivors blamed 3rd party interference (mother in law, sister-in-law and brother-in-law)
78%
Survivors had previously approached religious institutions or family members for help before approaching Government.
MENTAL ABUSE
70%
Perpetrators said they were survivors of verbal and emotional abuse
ASSAULT DENIAL
88%
Perpetrators denied ever physically assaulting the survivor
LACK OF PROSECUTION
20%
Out of the 20% that were initially interested in prosecution, 18% withdrew the case from court.
www.dsvrtlagos.org
©2017

We now had scientific data to give credence to the fact that religious institutions are sometimes first responders, especially for domestic violence. This was a positive and important information. It also made sense since the overwhelming majority of Nigerians identified themselves as members of one religion or the other, developing and maintaining close ties with other members of their religious communities in whose arms they were likely to find comfort in trying times. This therefore meant that we had to get the religious clerics on our side. We could no longer be viewing them as *the* enemy. This led to the developing of programmes aimed at engaging religious clerics about Sexual and GenderBased Violence, their roles, the provisions of the law, and the need for them to have interfaces with the government.

We developed materials targeted at Faith Based Institutions, and then aggressively went after them to build their capacity to appropriately respond to cases. This was done via trainings as well as sensitisation drives. One of the key objectives of these engagements was to strengthen the referral system between religious institutions and DSVRT.

It was not too long after the first set of trainings and engagements that we started to receive referrals from religious institutions. We also began to receive invitations to attend and *preach* our zero-tolerance message in the services and at Jumat. Of course, this was an opportunity to re-emphasize the position of the law and inform members of the various congregations of the various services offered by our team, as well as share our hotlines.

The issue of lack of evidence, particularly in domestic violence was brought to the fore as a result of this data analysis. We realised that the majority of the clients that reported did not have real evidence, medical reports, police reports, recording, or any form of evidence to corroborate their assertions. Abuse allegations could so easily, in the absence of evidence, devolve into a 'my word, against yours' affair that often goes nowhere in the court.

'You did it!' the victim would cry.

'I did not do anything!' the perpetuator would reply.

'But you did!' the victim cries again.

'Okay, where's your evidence?' the perpetuator dares. 'Provide evidence, or else it's my word against yours.'

But no one walks into a new day expecting to be abused, carrying equipment to record their trauma for safekeeping. Consequently,the victim would wilt, all their rage and pain and shame and rancour imploding within them.

In the absence of real evidence, case officers have had to deploy negotiation and mediation skills to ensure the survivor can access justice. In the rare instances where the survivor has evidence, it makes the process easier, as this gives him or her leverage at the mediation table, at the police station or even in court.

Even when the survivor has pictorial evidence, I have had certain abusers raise doubts about the genuineness or otherwise of the picture. Some have told me it is photoshop, makeup, or she is the one that hit her body or cut herself to frame him. These are allegations that technically cannot be ruled out until investigations are concluded.

This knowledge has made us change our tactics, messaging and engagement. We commenced informing people to document, to take pictures immediately the abuse occurs, back them up to their emails or share with someone else and ensure the case is reported at either the police station or hospitals.

The truth of the matter is that as responders, we need to continuously ensure domestic violence cases are handled like any other criminal case, which would therefore require evidence. This has been instrumental in helping survivors *build their cases.*

The findings of the data also revealed that majority of the survivors who reported domestic violence at the office were still interested in the relationship. They however wanted the abuse to stop.

They also wanted their abusive spouses to compulsorily undergo counselling, therapy, anger management; therefore, we had to adapt our services to include the provision of psychosocial therapy for alleged abusers. This was very successful in instances where the alleged abuser was willing to admit to the violence and was desirous of getting help.

Unfortunately, this is very rare as the data showed us that majority of the alleged abusers are in denial. Nonetheless, we ensure survivors and alleged abusers are aware of this service, and are encouraged to take advantage of the service.

CHAPTER 11

ESTABLISHING A MULTI- SECTORAL APPROACH

Coordinated Approach to Domestic and Sexual Violence

A Domestic and Sexual Violence Response Team can be defined as a collection of professional service providers and officials that respond essentially as a group, and in a timely fashion, to the various needs of domestic and sexual violence survivors. It is to encourage and create unprecedented levels of collaboration among professionals working to end Sexual and Gender-Based Violence in the State.

The most popular approaches used by other jurisdictions to deal with these problems is to engage in a coordinated effort that incorporates the wide range of professional disciplines who are involved in providing both the response and resources for domestic and sexual assault survivors within the community.

Whilst the Response Team is not the kind of panacea that will solve all of the problems that communities face in responding effectively to sexual and domestic assault, the Response Team provides a structure for coordinating the services offered by the various disciplines.

In other words, working together doesn't automatically guarantee success, but the alternative almost guarantees failure. Problems are not very likely to be solved when professionals operate only within the bounds of their own discipline, and engage in limited communication or cooperation with others.

Responding to Sexual and Gender-Based Violence requires a multidisciplinary approach, the primary responsibility of a Response Team is therefore to coordinate immediate response across responder agencies to disclosures of sexual and domestic assault.

An SGBV Response Team would primarily be saddled with the responsibility of providing immediate response, which would typically include making contact with survivors, providing medical evaluation and care, conducting a preliminary investigation, provide support crisis counselling, information and referral services, document and collect forensic and crime scene evidence as support, and provide information for survivor's families and friends.

As regards sexual assault, the goals of the Response Team should be two-fold. The first is to ensure survivors have prompt access to comprehensive immediate care, minimise the trauma they may experience, and encourage their use of community resources. The second is to facilitate the collection and documentation of evidence, as well as the rest of the actions required for a preliminary investigation, in a manner that is timely, thorough, and respectful to survivors. The hope is that this type of investigation will increase the likelihood that offenders will be prosecuted and held accountable.

For Domestic Violence, I recall that DSVRT's goal at its inception used to be to increase the number of physical assault cases that were reported at the police station and subsequently charged to court. However, over time, we realised that most survivors of domestic violence are not interested in pursuing justice through the criminal justice system. Most survivors want:

1. the beating to stop;
2. the abusive partner to be 'warned, 'threatened' and or 'shaken';
3. the case to be reported and for the abusive partner to be called to order;
4. an undertaking is signed by the abusive partner to desist from the[2] violent ways;
5. the police to 'pick him up', 'tortured in the cell for two days and released';
6. abusive partner should be compelled to receive counselling[3].

When the survivor is resolute, and no longer interested in the relationship, the needs are generally:

1. full custody of the child(ren) while the abusive partner provides maintenance;
2. The Restraining Order, preventing the abusive partner from coming close to the survivor, especially where the abusive partner has in time past, threatened that they would kill;
3. abusive partner to be forced to leave the house.

In essence, a Response Team should strive to ensure that victims of domestic violence are well informed of the various options available to them.

---

[2] **Actual words used by 60% of survivors**

[3] Findings revealed from analysis of DSVRT data

Looking at what has worked in Lagos State as a model for other states to replicate, there are certain institutions that are critical in the multi-disciplinary framework.

It is imperative that the Office of the Attorney General coordinates the efforts of the Response Team. The Attorney General, being the Chief Law Officer of the State, is saddled with the responsibility of ensuring access to justice; upholding the rule of law is critical in ensuring holistic support is provided to survivors of domestic and sexual violence. This would, by extension, include the relevant departments and agencies under the Ministry of Justice that have interface and interactions with survivors.

The police are also a critical player in this space, especially taking into cognisance that most times, the Police is usually the first port of call for survivors of Sexual and Gender Based Violence crimes. The police therefore play a very key and pivotal role in the success or otherwise of these cases.

The Ministry of Women Affairs & Poverty Alleviation (WAPA) is another important stakeholder, especially as the majority of the survivors of domestic and sexual violence are women. The Ministry can also serve as a first responder and provide mediation, psychological and psychosocial services for survivors of domestic violence. A critical contribution from the Ministry is the access to empowerment and skill acquisition programmes which are typically under its purview. The education system has proven to be one of the most sustainable means of shaping behavioural mindsets and it is for this reason, amongst others that the Ministry of Education is a critical partner in the coordination of response.

Of course, the government cannot by itself provide all the services survivors of domestic and sexual violence are in dire need of. This is one of the reasons why partnership with non-governmental organisations and civil society organisations that operate in this space is critical. The NGOs are entrenched in the community. They also serve as survivor advocates for their survivors and family members. Conversely, the Ministry of Health and the Primary HealthCare Board play a pivotal role in ensuring survivors are able to access medical assistance. The Ministry is also crucial in mainstreaming GBV services into the health sector—access to healthcare. The Ministry ensures that survivors of rape, domestic violence and child abuse receive treatment timeously at the State Hospitals. The Ministry, particularly the Primary HealthCare Board ensures that the State Sexual Assault Standing Order is strictly adhered to.

For states that have Sexual Assault Referral Centres (Rape Crisis Centre), this is an invaluable service that should be incorporated on the response team. Finally, the Media, the fourth estate of the realm is a critical team player as they enable survivors share their stories with a survivor centred approach. The media is also instrumental in serving as a pressure group on the relevant responder agencies to ensure that high- risk cases remain on the front burner and are brought to a logical conclusion. Finally, a coordinator is required to *coordinate* response across the various sectors. This would be the only task for this this individual. This person would need to have access to the key policymakers. Having a legal or social work background would be an added advantage. Finally, a coordinator is required to *coordinate* response across the various sectors.

CHAPTER 12

THE MAKING OF THE LAW

From Domestic and Sexual Violence Response Team to Domestic and Sexual Violence Agency

As a result of the massive support we had from the Lagos State Government and the increase in awareness about support services in the state, reported cases had more than doubled from 440 reported cases in 2016 to 1044 cases in 2017. We had started to take our place not just in Lagos, but indeed in Nigeria. We were gradually spreading the wings of our mission. Each person that managed to overcome barriers and lodge their reports— telling their stories—was a victory in itself.

They were on the verge, beckoning to the eagle of safety to fly them home. It was an enormous responsibility, fraught with challenges, but meaningful and satisfying too. With the amount of work and delivery of services to the people of Lagos State, it was evident to me that the Lagos State Domestic and Sexual Violence Response Team had indeed become a force to be reckoned with.

Furthermore, considering the sensitive nature of the cases handled by the DSVRT, there had arisen a need for the DSVRT to have a legal personality which must be conferred by law, as a juridical organisation, hence the need for an enabling law which would also confer much-needed credibility on the organisation. Enacting a law was also crucial to ensure the sustainability and institutionalisation of the initiative. The Law would therefore codify and strengthen the existing functions of DSVRT which I hoped would cement the structures we had put in place and drive sustainability.

This was an opinion that Mrs Omotilewa Ibirogba and I were totally in alignment with. I recall her motherly voice and her brows furrowed with wisdom and remembrance as she spoke. In her, it was easy to find strength and amiable energy, energy that came through when the days were daunting and overwhelming.

Thus, I drafted a Bill for A Law to Establish the Domestic and Sexual Violence Response Agency, Trust Fund and For Other Connected Purposes, 2017. The highlights of the Bill are as listed below:

1. **Section 1** provided for the establishment of an Agency to be known as the Lagos State Domestic and Sexual Violence Response Agency (referred to as "the Agency"), which shall be a body corporate with perpetual succession and a common seal; that may sue and be sued in its corporate name; and acquire, hold and dispose of any property or interest in property, movable or immovable for the purpose of carrying out its functions under this Law.

2. **Section 2** provided for the functions and powers of the Agency which shall be to:

    a. coordinate immediate response across community agencies to disclosures of sexual and domestic assault;

    b. foster effective, enduring public-private partnership for tackling Sexual and Gender-Based crimes in the State;

    c. acquire, deploy and maintain up-to-date technology which will, inter alia, enable victims to quickly access medical and legal assistance, aid in knowledge exchange; assist in coordinating work on cases, assist in obtaining quick access to case management tools; and also facilitate the provision of online services to victims of Sexual and Gender-Based Violence in the State;

d. assist prosecutors, as may be necessary, to secure the attendance of witnesses and offset exceptional and unexpected costs of litigation;

e. ensure continuous advocacy and sensitization programs for members of the public and targeted groups in the society;

f. implement support strategies to increase the capacity of responder agencies; make services more accessible to the public by raising awareness of social justice issues and participating in the development of sociolegal policies, laws and legal practices for the benefit of disadvantaged people; and

g. do such other things as may be necessary for the achievement of the foregoing objectives.

3. **Section 4** provided that there shall be a Governing Council for the Agency (referred to in this Law as "the Council") which shall consist of:

   a. a Chairman who shall be the Attorney-General and Commissioner for Justice Lagos State;

   b. the Director of the Directorate for Citizens' Rights;

   c. the Director of Public Prosecutions;

   d. the Director of the Office of the Public Defender;

   e. the Divisional Police Officers in the Family Support Units of the Nigerian Police Force;

   f. the Director in charge of Women Affairs in the Ministry of Women Affairs and Poverty Alleviation;

   g. the Coordinator of the Agency;

h. a member each of the Lagos State Judiciary presiding over the Family Courts, at Magistrate and High Court level;

i. the officer in Charge of Child Protection in the Ministry of Youth and Social Development;

j. the officer in charge of Reproductive Health and Nutrition at the Ministry of Health;

k. an officer of the Ministry of Education;

l. two representatives each of the Sexual Assault Referral Centres in Lagos State;

m. a representative each of credible media houses in operation in Lagos State;

n. four representatives of credible Non-Governmental Organisations whose membership shall in the opinion of the Council, assist with the promotion of ADR as a concept; and

o. two persons who are qualified legal practitioners of not less than ten (10) years post qualification.

4. **Section 14** provided that there is established a fund to be known as the Lagos State Domestic and Sexual Violence Response Trust Fund (referred to in this Law as "the Fund"), which shall be the depository of all monies received under this Law.

5. **Section 15** provided for Objective of the Trust Fund which shall be to - raise money through private and public contributions to ensure support services, establishments, resource materials, tools and equipment, and the institutional framework is in place to holistically address issues of Sexual and Gender Based Violence crimes in the State;

   a. pursue private, corporate, local, state, federal and international funding opportunities to accomplish the State's policy of ensuring the incidents of Sexual and Gender based Violence crimes is reduced to the barest minimum;

b. fund fully or in part, qualifying Government and NGO projects geared towards curbing incidents of Sexual and Gender-Based Violence as may be decided upon by the Board;

c. fund the training and retraining of members of the Lagos State Domestic and Sexual Violence Response Team as well as relevant agency personnel; and

d. provide immediate financial assistance to high-risk victims during their quest to justice either by providing transportation, relocation or any other form of allowance where necessary.

6. **Section 16** provided for the establishment of a Board of Trustees to be known as the Lagos State Domestic and Sexual Violence Response Trust Fund Board of Trustees (referred to in this Law as "the Board").

7. Furthermore, Section 21 provided that the functions of the Board shall be to:

   a. manage the Fund established under this Law and all other properties that may from time to time be vested in it for the benefit of the people of Lagos State;

   b. pay or reward any person for services rendered or to be rendered to it;

   c. pay and discharge out of the Trust property all expenses properly incurred by it or by any of its members; and

   d. ensure at all times in the management of the Fund that the Fund shall have sufficient money and materials to offer support

> for the fight against Sexual and Gender-Based Violence crimes and the assistance of survivors of such crimes in the State.

On 2 June 2017, the Memorandum forwarding the draft bill was submitted to the Honourable Attorney General for his perusal and for Governor's approval.

The bill was subsequently forwarded to the Directorate of Legislative Drafting for their input before forwarding same to the Governor for Executive Council's consideration.

Fortunately for me, I had earlier briefed Mr David Kehinde in the Directorate of Legislative Drafting about the bill and he had given me some invaluable advice on how to proceed. I was glad when the file was sent to him for his attention. After several meetings, the bill had been 'murdered' and reborn.

I was pleased with the outcome. More powers had been conferred upon the Agency, other innovations had been introduced and as is customary, the Bill was returned to the Director of Legislative Drafting. After several meetings with the Director, the bill was forwarded to the Attorney General for his approval and onward transmission to the Governor.

Unfortunately, the process identified above took approximately a year to accomplish, and we had now approached the end of Governor Ambode's administration. Despite the delays and times when I felt I should just give up, I felt that it would be to the administration's credit if the bill was passed and so, I kept following up on the file, until one fateful day, I was eventually able to lay my hand on the file.

It was a large file, cream-colored and hardbacked and I hesitated to look at it. What it contained could make or break months, even years of effort. I drew in a deep breath and steeled my stomach, then applied my eyes. As I read the comments of the Hon. Attorney General on the sticky note on the file to the Permanent Secretary, I felt my heart break into pieces, into restless pieces that yearned and begged for resolution. I felt so disappointed, and I just felt at that point perhaps, it was not meant to be.

Maybe it was the pregnancy hormones, maybe it was because I felt I had wasted a whole year of my life chasing this and now it appeared it was not going to be a reality. But at the time, the world seemed to dissolve and I felt in close existential contact with the pains of my being, the failures and the catastrophes highlighted as though in relief. I remember walking out of the office, feeling the cold arms of grief hug my soul. I remember wanting to cry.

I moved on and hoped that the bill would be revived. Sometimes, it takes everything you have to give to keep this sort of hope alive, and I assure you the onslaught of despair had been merciless. Sometimes, it takes everything you've got to keep your feet planted to the earth, traipsing forward, however seemingly snail-like and discouraging the pace. But I was determined not to allow the drawback about the bill to deter me from fulfilling our precious and most noble mandate, and striving to make progress in this area.

Hope sauntered back into the vision when Governor Sanwo-Olu assumed office. It was 2019, a year that brimmed with political energy and anticipation. Governor Sanwo-Olu came into office and appointed Mr Moyosore Onigbanjo, SAN as the Attorney General and Commissioner for Justice. Shortly after he assumed office, he requested to see members of DSVRT. He was, however, especially desirous of meeting the Director of Citizens Rights and myself.

At our meeting, we discussed several issues including the effectiveness or otherwise of our Sex Offenders Register and it was agreed that to ensure full implementation, a law needed to be enacted for this purpose. The Hon.

Attorney General expressed this as one of his cardinal objectives for his administration, ending or reducing the commission of Sexual and Gender-Based Violence to the barest minimum. I'll leave you to imagine the depth of my joy, how far down my belly it reached, how my nerves tickled and my soul smiled.

It is important to reference this meeting, which was indeed a defining moment in my career as the activities that would follow this encounter shook me to my very foundation (This would be documented in another book). I was then tasked to present a draft bill on the Sex Offenders Register.

This concept was of course not alien to me, especially leveraging the research I embarked upon while proposing the Executive Order on Sex Offenders Register. In a sense, a good measure of my life's work involved me interning for this opportunity. I seized it with gladness. This moment also presented an opportunity to strengthen and include innovations, including different tiers of sexual offenses.

As a result of the urgency expressed by the Attorney General, a draft bill for the establishment of a Sex Offenders register was ready within a day. It was shared with the Attorney General who then forwarded it to the Directorate of Legislative Drafting for their input. Some days later, I went to follow up on the file and I met with the Director of Legislative Drafting, Mrs Ogunmola. She wondered why we were proposing another bill as she felt it could be merged with the existing bill, seeking to establish the Domestic and Sexual Violence Agency. We went on to meet with the AG and she reiterated her opinion and was asked to proceed accordingly.

The two files were assigned to an officer who unfortunately did not have a background of the previous file; neither did the person understand the vision of DSVRT and what the bill sought to achieve. Given this, the bill was watered-down and almost lost its essence. In all honesty, this was another trying moment for me. If something needed to be done, then it needed to be done right, and to the fullest possible degree. This has always been my belief. But beyond that, the vision of DSVRT was a critical one; the consequences of cutting corners and permitting unneeded elbow room to perpetrators would be borne upon real people living real lives, enduring conditions no one would wish upon their enemy.

Huge and sweeping successful reforms may often seem like white elephant projects with seemingly outlandish ideas to some people, and when you have no choice but to collaborate with such people as is often the case, it is key to engage as though it is an opportunity to transmute their conviction. This was a lesson I learnt the hard way as I had often engaged the officer believing that she understood the vision behind the bill but was just being difficult, and this only led to further frustration on my part which took a toll on my emotional wellness. I had to accept what was given to me. What other options did I have? I saw the experience as one where you recognise the need for making little trade-offs in life, if success must be attained.

As a result of this, there were several meetings which unfortunately delayed progress. And then, a new Director of Legislative Drafting was appointed in the person of Mrs Derinsola Olanrewaju.

With Mrs Olanrewaju in the picture, we commenced renewed conversations around the bill which had now been merged and another senior counsel, whom I refer to as my Angel, Mrs Tomi Bodunde was tasked with seeing the bill through. I call her my angel because of her unyielding support, unwavering commitment, and wholehearted belief in this project. To me, she was a Godsent, for there was no other way for me to describe the manner in which she came to us, and the way in which she wielded her position and abilities to further the vision.

Unfortunately, during this period, other bills which were deemed high priority surfaced and so we suffered delay. Nonetheless, I kept pushing and then finally, the bill was forwarded to the Honourable Attorney General for his approval.

During that period, there was an undocumented policy discouraging the establishment of new agencies, due to overhead expenditures and so a justification had to be made for why we sought to establish "another" Agency.

At this time, May 2020, there was a national focus on Sexual and Gender-Based Violence, the State of Emergency had been declared by the Governor's Forum and other States appeared more responsive and committed to tackling the issue as it concerned them in their respective States. To borrow Charles Dickens' famous words, 'it was the best of times, it was the worst of times, it was the age of wisdom... it was the epoch of belief...'

There was therefore no better time for this bill to have been proposed and pushed out. The rationale highlighted the various innovations of the state in formulating policies and enacting laws geared towards protecting the rights of the vulnerable. For it was a good thing, that the state was recognising its role in the protection of the vulnerable and coming into it. The rationale also underscored the important role the DSVRT, since its establishment in 2014, has been able to fulfil in ensuring survivors can access service, support and justice. It was no mere feat and the government acknowledged this, thankfully.

Furthermore, the rationale reiterated, per international best practice, the aim to have a 'one-stop shop' solution with key government and responder representatives (social workers, counsellors, criminologists, and legal) in the Agency, while the Agency's office would be decentralised across the divisions of the state to grant easy access to services for residents.

And then leveraging the current national outrage against incidents of Sexual and Gender-Based Violence, it was believed that that was indeed the best time to consolidate on our gains and create institutions to appropriately prevent and respond to Sexual and Gender-Based Violence crimes in Lagos.

We also underscored the fact that the team was already in existence, with an appropriate budgetary line and as such we were not seeking to create a new Agency per se, but rather, to strengthen the existing structures. Conceptually, this can be likened to a tree, with roots already lodged deep in the soil. We were going to provide more space and better conditions for the proper unfurling of its branches, so that it may bear fruit. And as the tree grew, and its branches stretched to brush the edges of the sky, it grew sturdier, firmer. This was the dream.

The bill was approved by Mr Governor for consideration by the Executive Council and it was subsequently considered by the Executive Council and approved as to be forwarded to the House of Assembly and then committed to the House Committee on Women Affairs and Poverty Alleviation and Job Creation, ably chaired by Hon. Mojisola Alli-Macaulay.

On 9 December 2020, we were invited to the public hearing of the bill. It was warm and sunny. As is customary, the stakeholders submitted memoranda comprising salient issues which they felt was critical and had not yet been addressed in the bill. Issues including the provision of support services for persons with disabilities who are also survivors were proposed as well as adequate funding to ensure sustained sensitisation of the public about these vices and ensure appropriate response to incidents.

The idea for specialised police force to investigate Sexual and Gender-Based Violence crimes was also suggested.

It was indeed a great day and we were filled with hope that this Bill would soon be passed into law.

I was informed that the Committee would lay the report before the House of Assembly sometime in February. Unfortunately, I was not able to physically participate. I however joined via the live stream. It wasn't an easy meeting, that one. I came into it armed with hopes and expectations, but fear still lingered in my heart. Several times, I and the team had come to the verge of success and had been held back by some vague, indeterminate grapnel. In this particular meeting, my fears prevailed. Some contentious sections were added which did not augur well with Honourable Members and so the bill was stepped down. We suffered a great setback as we had lost time.

The Hon. Attorney General once again got involved with a view to providing clarity as to the essence of the bill which was primarily to establish the Domestic and Sexual Violence Agency and also the Sex Offenders Register.

The Report was subsequently presented on 6 June 2021 for Second Allotted Day. This time, the report sailed through Second Reading and was awaiting Third Reading. On 15 June 2021, the bill was presented for Third Reading and it was passed by the House of Assembly.

Mr Governor gave his assent to the Law establishing the Lagos State Domestic and Sexual Violence Agency on 20 September 2021, in commemoration of Domestic and Sexual Violence Awareness Month.

This bill garnered immense support from the Governor, Mr Babajide Sanwo-Olu, who has been supportive from the inception of His Administration; the Honourable Attorney General and Commissioner for Justice, Mr Moyosore Onigbanjo (SAN), who has genuinely believed in this cause; the Solicitor General and Permanent Secretary, Ms Titilayo Shitta-Bey; Hon. Mojisola Alli-Macaulay, as well as other distinguished members of the House of Assembly, including Hon. Temitope Adewale and Hon. Gbolahan Yishawu; the Learned Head of Service, Mr Hakeem Muri-Okunola, a keen supporter of DSVRT from the early days, and one of the active mentors of the Kings Club, and immense support from other key stakeholders across the State Executive Council.

The passion and corresponding tenacity of the First Lady, Dr (Mrs) Claudiana Ibijoke Sanwo-Olu on tackling issues of Sexual and Gender-Based Violence is unprecedented. She has indeed walked the talk in so many ways. She took time to understand the journey so far and provided assistance in strengthening the coordination mechanism in the state; including donating utility vehicles to responder agencies, influencing the establishment of the Sexual Intervention Fund, and overall, helping to push the agenda of a Sexual and Gender-Based Violence free state. Her contribution towards ensuring the bill became a law cannot be taken for granted. Indeed, nothing is impossible where there is political will.

On the day the bill was signed into law, what however caught me by surprise, was the on-the-spot announcement by Mr Governor, Babajide Sanwo-Olu, appointing myself as the pioneer Executive Secretary. While I had deep down desired this position, my years of experience in the public service had also somewhat dampened my expectations and I had resigned myself to believing that getting the law signed was a good enough legacy to attain. I deeply appreciate Mr Governor for the trust bestowed on me, and I do not take it for granted.

What started out as an idea, inside a small office with a table and two chairs, a coordinator and a volunteer, has now morphed into a full-blown Agency with over 70 staff. This transition process has been nothing short of inspiring, and humbling.

CHAPTER 13

MOVING FORWARD

The hands of time, having turned as though in mad haste, have led us to this here and now, this place in the road so far up the mountain, affording a unique vantage point from where we can see that so much has been done and yet so much remains to be done. The years have drifted by as though in a daze. Seasons have come and gone like dreams and now, I am gifted the gift of reminiscence. The past seven years, we have been able to build from scratch, a government institution that enjoys goodwill and acceptability from members of the public. We have been accountable to the people, our major stakeholders even as we have strived to build an institution, the engine room of coordination of response in Lagos State.

When I look back, I am filled with mixed feelings; feelings with the colour riot inherent in a rainbow. On one part, I am filled with so much joy and pride, soft and warm emotions, on account of what we have been able to accomplish in such a short period of time. It is no small task, giving one's soul to a cause, garnering the support of the right people, waking up daily to *do* courage, despite the many moments of fear and weakness. It is a way of living that can be deeply meaningful, but also stressful in myriad ways. This is why on the other hand, I feel a bit of regret for not taking the time to celebrate the big and not-so-big wins, for not taking necessary breathers and always scurrying off to the next project, policy or programme.

Sometimes I wonder, maybe we did too much within such a short period of time? Perhaps, we should have phased out the different innovations and reforms proposed? Perhaps we should have been more meticulous with the pace, acknowledging that the journey we were embarking on was nearly inexhaustible, and could perhaps use the deliberateness of wise, old tortoise.

What's next? Is there any innovation or idea that has not yet been explored? What else can be done to ensure improved coordination amongst responder agencies?

These thoughts cross my mind every now and then but instead of giving in and becoming complacent, with each new case I handle, I realise that though we have done quite a lot in such a short period of time, there remains much more yet to be done. In fact, at times it seems as though we have just scratched the surface, like what one does to an itch.

Our initiatives have to be properly institutionalised and fully implemented. This is critical for sustained development and a launchpad for scaling across every corner of Lagos, while being a template for other states, and I dare say countries to adopt from.

I have always been a firm believer that it is not enough for one to have policies, which have the tendency of gathering dust on the shelves, we need individuals, and institutions that would drive those policies and ensure they come alive and effective. The usefulness of a policy lies mostly in how much pragmatic utility it had, and how it could make better the lives of the people for whom it is formulated. Policies too need enlivening breaths and activator mechanisms, for them to flourish.

What I have been privileged to do is create an institution from scratch and then midwife it into full term birth so that it has a life of its own and can continue to grow and be nurtured. It can bloom in all the best ways, like the proverbial tree planted by the riverside.

I have seen first-hand, the potency of policies and how they can work. People that had lost hope, lost the zeal to live are encouraged to bloom again. I have seen how people's lives and destinies can be changed if the right policies are in place and being fully implemented.

Conceptualising, researching, formulating, and implementing public policy, and then actual public service; that's my calling. It's what I was born to do, serve humanity and being a true Merchant of Hope. And so, for as long as I am able to live this life purpose of mine, I see it as my own contribution to nation building, to ensure the different policy initiatives and the laws come alive, and are enforced to the letter; so help me, God.

CHAPTER 14

LESSONS LEARNT

Below, in no particular order are some of the lessons I have learnt during the course of my work at the DSVRT:

i. With political will, nothing is impossible;

ii. For optimum impact, the State Governors have to champion the cause of ending Sexual and GenderBased Violence:

iii. Funding, funding, funding. You can have all the passion, drive and zeal, without funding, the passion would be extinguished;

iv. The process of introducing innovations has to be participatory, the stakeholders have to be involved. This is critical to sustainability and ownership;

v. Not every survivor/victim wants to be helped, and that's okay. Let them at least know that help is available, should they ever feel the need to reach out;

vi. To build a government institution that enjoys public goodwill takes time and deliberate efforts. Perception is critical. You need to care about what the public thinks, and you need to respect public opinion;

vii. Nothing is impossible. If it hasn't been done, it's because the people at the helm of affairs do not deem it expedient;

viii. Institutions are important, but so is leadership. We need strong, competent leaders who would drive institutions

ix. When starting an initiative, there might not be funding. Don't give up, if you keep putting in the effort, at some point, your work will begin to speak for you and then the funding would come:

x. For the purpose of sustainability, responder agencies must have an appropriate budget line for response (either prevention or remedial) to Sexual and Gender-Based Violence;

xi. Everybody wants to feel relevant. Everyone wants to be carried along. Everybody wants to have a sense of belonging. Everybody wants to feel part of the process. If this is not happening, there would be a combination of internal and external dissent which could lead to division and strife if not managed properly;

xii. Working with the right people is critical for the successful implementation of an innovation;

xiii. If a person takes an idea conceived by you, there is a natural tendency to feel contempt towards such a person. The most important thing is that the idea is actualised properly and the greater good benefits;

xiv. It pays to remain focused on what you have been set up to do lest you become jack of trade, and master of none;

xv. To appropriately respond to Sexual and Gender Based Violence, certain institutions particularly the Police Force, despite being a federal institution, have to be in perfect synergy with State institutions to ensure maximum efficiency and productivity.

APPENDIX

In the past seven years, DSVRT has taken a three-pronged approach in addressing Sexual and Gender-Based Violence in Lagos State:

- Provision of Medical services
- Awareness and Sensitisation
- Quick dispensation of justice

In the course of our response, DSVRT observed several challenges and subsequently proposed the following innovations:

SEXUAL VIOLENCE

1. **Lack of adequate access to medical care for survivors of sexual assaults at the grassroots level**

   Response:

   - Launched the Lagos State Sexual Assault Standing Order (first of its kind in Nigeria) to be used at all state health facilities. The Standing Order designates sexual assault as emergencies.
   - Developed and Launched Sexual Assault Examination Kit (Rape Kit) for PHCs, first of its kind in Nigeria.
   - DSVRT facilitates and pays for the provision of tests.
   - Facilitated the upgrade of all comprehensive Primary Healthcare Training of Health Officials drawn for all health

workers drawn from all comprehensive PHCs on Sexual Assault Management.

2. **Lack of data depicting trends and possible reasons for why people perpetrate sexual assaults**

   Response:

   - Commissioned a detailed research in all prison facilities in Lagos State on sex convicts and inmates awaiting trial for SEXUAL AND GENDER BASED VIOLENCE cases
   - Results of the research disclosed that 80.9% of the inmates were abused as children implying that they had become sexually active at an early age. This illustrates the 'abused abuser' trend.
   - 89% of them were always under the influence of alcohol, while 10.9% were under the influence of hard drugs.
   - *NONE OF THE INMATES SAMPLED SAID THEY WERE AROUSED BY WHAT THEIR SURVIVOR WORE.* This further debunks the myth that the mode of dressing is a 'reason' why people rape or sexually abuse others.
   - The results of this research have guided our advocacy and sensitisation campaigns, and emphasis is also placed on the boy child.

3. **Low Awareness of what to do if a person has been sexually abused**

   Response:

   - Developed a Rape Manual that highlights steps to take if one has been raped. This has been distributed to Secondary school students, higher institutions, hospitals, churches, mosques, civil society organisations and the police stations for survivors.

- The manual also highlights the different roles of each Responder Agency and what to expect upon contact.
- Created a section on the DSVRT website which shares a step by step guide on the next actions a survivor should take after an incident has occurred.

4. **Unwillingness of the survivor to go through the legal process due to lack of information and disbelief in the system**

Response:

- Early engagement with the survivors to sensitise them of their rights and the need to prosecute such cases in court.
- Early engagement with the Divisional Police Officers and the Investigative Police Officers to ensure that the case is properly investigated and the defendant is promptly charged to court.
- Accompanying the survivor to the Police Station, hospital to ensure that everything required by law to sustain a conviction is done.

5. **Investigation and evidence gathering**

Response:

- Equipped the Gender Desk officers and Police prosecutors with copies of the 3 relevant laws- namely Childs's Rights Law, 2007, Protection against Domestic Violence Law, 2007 and Criminal Law of Lagos State, 2011.

6. **The rise of Sexual assault and Harassment on campus**

Response:

- Commenced our Sexual Assault Prevention Drive for Higher Institutions- Sharing preventive tips, the role of the by-stander and how to stay safe, and the concept of consent—putting the responsibility back on the male.

CHILD ABUSE/ CHILD PROTECTION:

1. Increase in reports of child abuse

   Response:

   - *DSVRT* drafted and facilitated the ratification of the Executive Order on Sex Offender Register and Mandated Reporting policy that now makes it mandatory for all officers in child centred institutions, to report actual or suspected cases of child abuse to the relevant authorities. DSVRT then proceeded to train over 1,800 *Mandated Reporters* on Child's Rights Law, Child Abuse, and their role as *Mandated Reporters* according to the Executive Order. The training was done on a rotational basis for all officers drawn from the 6 Education Districts.
   - DSVRT developed a Mandated Reporter Manual as well as posters which were distributed at the various trainings.
   - DSVRT commenced its *Safeguarding the Rights of a Child* workshops for Primary and Secondary school students on Child Abuse, Child's Rights and responsibilities, self-defence, how to avoid being a survivor of sexual abuse and how to preserve evidence when physically or sexually assaulted. The training was done on a rotational basis for over 4,500 students drawn from the six Education Districts.
   - DSVRT developed a colourful textbook called *Safeguarding the Rights of a Child (STRAC)*, with pictures in a language that children can understand, relate with and appreciate. It was also developed to encourage a reading culture for children.
   - At the point of establishment of DSVRT, Lagos State had not formulated a Child Protection Policy. This was a major stumbling block in enforcement.

- Consequently, DSVRT facilitated the drafting and ratification of the Executive Order prescribing the Lagos State Safeguarding and Child Protection Policy which was ratified by His Excellency, the Governor of Lagos State, first of its kind in Nigeria.
- To ensure strict compliance with the Child Protection Policy, DSVRT commenced Multi-Agency Trainings for all *Designated Safeguarding Child Protection Officers* and ensured posters and copies of the policies were distributed.
- In a bid to ensure parents are not left out, we have commenced the Parents Association Conference on Safeguarding and Child Protection and we have also developed resource materials for parents to refer to after the conference.

2. **Low awareness of the consequences of the act and multi-faceted effects of Sexual and GenderBased Violence generally acts**

Response:

- DSVRT has organised Road Walks/market rallies have been held in key areas where these acts are the most prevalent in—Ikeja, Alimosho, Mushin and Lagos Island. We have increased awareness about the ills of these crimes in these areas and support services available to survivors.
- Media campaigns—mounting of billboards in prevalent areas, production and distribution of radio jingles in English and indigenous languages.
- Co-Producers of Unspoken Program, a live programme produced and aired on Silverbird TV that shows different facets of SEXUAL AND GENDER BASED VIOLENCE and support services available to survivors.

DOMESTIC VIOLENCE

1. **Dearth of information about the provisions of the Protection against Domestic Violence Law, 2007**

   Response:

   - Developed booklets, pamphlets and other resource materials on Domestic Violence.

2. **Who to contact/how to get help**

   Response:

   - DSVRT launched its website with the 'Online chat' option. Individuals can now report cases online, and most importantly, chat with psychologists who are available to provide psychosocial therapy.
   - Access to direct counselling with trained professionals via our toll free line- 0800-0333-333
   - Provision of legal advisory services via our social media platforms– Facebook, Email, Twitter and DSVRT's website.

3. **Lack of Enforcement of the Provisions of the Protection against Domestic Violence Law, 2007**

   Response:

   - Conducted trainings for over 220 police officers on the admissibility of evidence, application of the relevant laws, and the role of the police in enforcing the Prevention against Domestic Violence Law, 2007.

- Facilitated the upgrade of 8 Divisional Police Stations to house Family Support Units, thereby increasing the capacity of police personnel to handle Sexual and Gender-Based Violence cases.
- Conducted trainings for the judiciary on the law, and the applicability of same
- Drafted and facilitated the endorsement of the Practice Directions of the Protection against Domestic Violence Law, 2019 by the Chief Judge of Lagos State.

4. **Absence of provision of counselling and healing services for Survivors of Domestic Violence**

Response:

- Created a Support and Healing Group for
- Survivors of Domestic Violence, the first of its kind in Nigeria
- Support and Healing Group for children who have witnessed Intimate Partner Violence to be able to heal from their ordeal
- Individual therapeutic sessions for survivors and children
- Provision of anger management service for survivors and abusers

5. **Lack of Empowerment schemes tailored for Survivors of Domestic and Sexual Violence**

Response:

- Established the Lagos State Domestic and Sexual Violence Trust Fund to provide financial assistance to survivors who seek to relocate or women who need to be empowered so that they gain financial independence from their abusers.

OTHER INSTITUTIONAL REFORMS

1. **Lack of dedicated toll free lines to report cases**

   Response:

   - The first step to this initiative brought about the using of a short code which was approved by Nigerian Communications Commission, developed for reporting of Sexual and Gender Based Violence cases in Lagos State.
   - By dialling *6820# or sending an sms to 6820 with a keyword *e.g., child abuse*, users will be fed information on steps to take for the respective case (rape, child abuse, domestic violence). A report would also be lodged and forwarded to the appropriate law enforcement, agency or Ministry.
   - The aim of this innovation is to ensure that survivors of all forms of abuse would be able to reach out to the appropriate agencies and receive timely information about what to do, but most importantly, where to go to receive assistance.

2. **Lack of Direct contact with Lagos State residents for sensitisation and awareness purposes.**

   Response:

   - Commenced six months community engagement campaign in areas where reporting is most prevalent. The forms of engagement include door to-door campaigns, engagement of market men and women, traditional rulers, brethren in places of worships, salons, spas, marriage registries, persons in hospitals, street campaigns, etc. market rallies, engagement of students in schools and vocational centres

- Flowing from above, it is expected that a minimum of 2 million residents at the first instance would either have been impacted directly or indirectly.

3. **The paucity of information education materials for both advocacy and response.**

- Development of educational materials for members of the public–

  i. What You Must Know About Domestic Violence,

  ii. What You Must Know About Child Abuse,

  iii. Safeguarding the Rights of a Child (pictorial book for children).

I was also privileged to have drafted and proposed policy documents for responder agencies, including Protocol Response to Domestic Violence, Best Practices for Investigating and Prosecuting Domestic Violence, Lagos State Sexual Assault Standing Order, Standard Operating Procedure on the provision of Psychosocial Support for Survivors.

FROM SURVIVORS…

It all started in 2015. I ran out of my house due to domestic violence. I took my baby to my mum in Enugu so I could take up a new job, settle down and then bring him back home. Somehow, my husband managed to bring back my baby to Lagos without my consent. I almost passed out when I heard about his move.

Devastated and troubled, going around looking for a solution, a friend of mine gave me Lola's contact. I spoke with her and she invited me to her office in Alausa, Lagos. During our meeting, she was very welcoming. She gave me time to pour my heart out without interruption. She listened to me very well and assured me that her office will help with my case. I was devastated.

She gave me a letter to OPD Lagos, where OPD leadership intervened in my case and my child was brought back to me that same day I reported to OPD. I was amazed and stunned at how the Lagos State Government was efficient and effective. Thanks to Lola as her dedication and her constant show of genuine love and care helped me a lot.

Fast forward to 2017, I had to report to Lola's office again because my husband's abuses were getting out of hand. Her office helped instantly, to secure a restraining order from the magistrate court. The court later summoned my husband where the case was handled professionally. She and her staff followed up with the whole process, providing real-time feedback to me. I was never at any time during this whole process kept in the dark. They ensured that I followed all the court proceedings and that I got the judgement I deserved. Her advice and professional diligence in handling my case was impeccable. She recommended I go for counselling afterwards.

A few years later, when my husband's constant abuses were getting worse, I reached out to her office again for help knowing that her office is one place I can get all the help I need. Lola listened to me again without any concerns on my persistent visits to her office.

This time, my husband abducted my kids from my nanny on their way to school. As I quickly reached her on the matter, she took charge and assured me that my kids will be returned to me.

She summoned me and we went to a police station to report the case and seek assistance. With her help, the family unit of the police station intervened and my kids were returned to me within two days.

The day I saw my kids again after their father took them away from me was one of the happiest days of my life. I cried so much but was also filled with joy. I wondered what could have been my fate if Lola and her office did not intervene.

Thank you so much, Lola. The professionalism you show when handling my case is quite commendable. Her team is also great. I saw the way she interacts with them and they mirrored her character when dealing with me. I can say she is a good mentor to the young people working with her.

I have no doubt that Lola and her team will continue to provide help and assistance to women especially, those who have no place to find succour when they find themselves in an abusive relationship.

Well done in all you do and I wish you the very best in your future endeavours.

End

I am a woman of many colours with high hopes, marvellous dreams and aspirations. I am a preacher of love, peace and family.

I was 26 years old when I met this young man of my dreams, and he was 28 years then. I fell in love with his loving, caring, and hardworking spirit. He loved me so much that he could starve for me to eat what I desired when I went visiting, He was all over me. He was unstable financially but he had big dreams and was really working hard at that time to achieve his goals I was blindfolded with the love.

I met his mum, his dad is late, and he proposed marriage after two years of courtship while we were dating, I saw traces of aggression and obsession but I thought it was true love. I felt I was in my late twenties and my friends were already married and having kids. I thought the love will override all that.

While we were dating, he slapped me twice during n hot argument between us about him still seeing his ex-girlfriend, but he later broke down, apologized and begged never to raise his hands again. I thought I overreacted and was jealous, so I forgave him. Some weeks to our wedding, we were playing Ludo board game and I won three times successively. He got angry and almost beat me up. Later he apologised and we moved on.

We got married and I got pregnant. Then I notice he was avoiding me for some months. He started complaining about my food, my stature the shape of my stomach, my legs, and all. He was irritated at the sight of me. He started staying out late and sleeping out, abandoning his food. He doesn't allow me to touch his phone anymore. He shouts and screams at me when he wants to talk to me. I couldn't report him to anyone, it was too early, and the marriage was just six months old.

One evening, he came home very late and all messy. I started asking questions but to my greatest surprised he slapped me and pushed me down, he didn't even mind my condition, and he pounced on me, and tore my shirt and forcefully removed my short and pant and had his way, I was crying and shouting, he didn't care. And when he was done, he took his bath, dressed up and went out. He came home the next day, he didn't apologise. He just greeted me and walked past me.

All the while, I was broken, bitter and frustrated in my condition, I had series of injuries, my neighbours will ask questions but I ignore or tell a lie. I didn't have any friend around me, he never allowed it. I wasn't close to my family; we only talk on the phone. And whenever I want to visit, he objects completely, he doesn't want a third party, no family, no friend—that is his slogan. I had to keep quiet. I got so scared of him I thought about my condition and I just endured the pain. He didn't want me to work for anyone, so I decided to do business I opened a viewing centre and game centre, when he realised that I was making a lot of money. He will just come to the shop, ask me for a huge sum of money and if I refused, he will beat me up and forcefully take my bag.

All along, he kept on changing jobs; I was taking care of the home. I remembered sometimes ago when our house rent was due and I couldn't save enough money to pay. He told me to call my mother and beg for a huge sum of money. I refused to lie to my mum and all of a sudden, he took a bottle, smashed it and was ready to cut me up, I was so scared I had to do it. My mother later sent the money we paid the rent and he took the balance with force, I developed high blood pressure in pregnancy. On several occasions I went to the hospital, the doctors and matrons will call him to tell him that I would be hospitalised and he will tell them never to do that, instead he will yell at me on the phone and threaten me. I also had stomach ulcer on two or three occasions I tried to report him to two of our pastors but I didn't have the nerve to explain how he use to beat me up. After reporting him, he will come back home and give me the beating of my life. He pushed me down countless times during pregnancy, on a particular night, I was bleeding and he left me on the floor till morning before I called a neighbour to take me to the hospital, still, I couldn't talk.

One day he came home and got angry that I couldn't call him to ask how he was fairing, he tore my clothes and pushed me out. A neighbour saw me and went to report him to his elder brother who was not too far away from the house. That is how his mother got to know. She later begged me and pleaded on his behalf still he didn't stop.

Because of my health status, I couldn't have a natural birth, I had my first boy through caesarean section I pulled through and bounce back to my normal daily activities I decided that if I would stay in the marriage, I will not give birth to another child. So, I started channelling all my emotions and pains to my job. I got a teaching job and in the evening, I go to the shop. I thought that would help me, but no, it didn't.

He will come to the school and disgrace me, come to the shop and beat me up because I was trying to keep my money and using it for the upkeep of our son and the family.

He expects that I should go and make the money and be giving it to him.

After five years, he called my mum and told my mum that he is not interested in marrying me again because I don't always allow him to have sex with me and he wants another child. After so much persuasion, my mum encouraged me to get pregnant again and that it's better for me to give birth before I clocked forty and that he has promised to change his ways if I agree.

I thought about it and I had a serious conversation with him and he promised to change his ways. So I gave in after some months I got pregnant immediately I informed him and was expecting that he will take me for antenatal. I stayed four months without any visit to the hospital, I fell sick; meanwhile, he got a new job and a better salary. He doesn't come home regularly, he started keeping late nights again and he refused to give me money to go to the hospital. I had to stop work, I couldn't go to the shop.

I was at home for months, weak and sick. My son was not regular in school anymore because I couldn't walk long distance there is no one to take him to school.

One day, when I was seven months pregnant. I had to call my mum and she sent some money for me to go to the hospital. He came home that night and beat me up blue black. I almost passed out he scratched my face, pulled some of my braids off and bit me with his teeth all over my body. I had several marks on my body. And he left the house.

A neighbour quickly came knocking immediately, when she saw me she quickly called a nurse nearby and I was attended to. He came home after two days and assumed everything is fine. It went on like that until my pregnancy was 10 months old, I was already due, and the doctors have booked me for a caesarean section and he said I will rather have a natural birth, he insisted that I wait and my blood pressure was high, labour didn't come. One morning, he was not around, and I almost collapsed inside, I was feeling very uncomfortable, so I called my neighbour and she helped me to the hospital, it was from the hospital that I called my mum, but it was late, she couldn't come the same day, she came the next day and the doctor asked us to go pack the baby things and come back for admission in two days.

When he saw my mum, he was shocked, my mother asked him for the deposit of the caesarean section and he said he doesn't have money, my mum called his mother and she later sent some money to him. He still insisted he doesn't have money, but he later dropped part of the deposit.

While we were going to the hospital he stayed back home, he said he needs to rest. I was admitted for two days to normalize my blood pressure before the operation. He didn't come. I was asked to call him to come and sign the form and donate some blood since my blood sample is not in the blood bank and I need two pints before the operation can commence.

He came and signed the form for the operation to be done but he said that he can't donate blood. The operation had to be delayed for two days before the blood was gotten from a private blood bank.

My mother wheeled me into the theatre, my first son slept in the hospital premises for 10 days. I had another baby boy and some complications. I was reacting to some of the injections I was given I couldn't breathe well so I was placed on oxygen for three days, I couldn't carry my baby until the fifth day. I was in great pains and very bitter. He came to the hospital and when he discovered that I had a boy, he said he wanted a girl, and didn't carry the baby, he insulted my mother and the nurses around because they scolded him for what he said.

On the eighth day, we left the hospital and named the baby, at night he came home late and was asking me questions, I was staring at him and he got angry, he just pushed me down and I fell and started bleeding. My stitches were soaked with blood. It was late, he said he can't go to the hospital he almost beat my mum up because she insisted that he opens the door because he locked the door as usual and increased the volume of the television set. It was obvious he was influenced by something. His eyes were so red and his steps unstable. In the morning my mother took me to the hospital. I was asked to come to the hospital twice in a week. He said he can't take me so I have to take a cab and bike to get there. My baby was two weeks old and I was still bleeding. Meanwhile my immediate senior sister is a doctor in the University College Hospital, Ibadan. So I called her and explained my health status. He advised that I should be admitted again and treated but the father of my children said he doesn't have money. I waited till the third week and he still said he can't afford any treatment. My baby was exactly three weeks old and my stitch was bringing out pus and blood, so it was very painful to feed the baby. That morning, I was quickly rushed to UCH, Ibadan he said I should take him with me that, he doesn't have time.

So, I took him with me to Ibadan. I just packed few things and we left. I spent three weeks in Ibadan and he never showed up. I was wheeled into the theatre and re-stitched. It was a painful experience. I was discharged the fourth week, and I came back to my mother's house in Lagos. When my baby was six weeks old, his mum started calling, and on one occasion she ordered me to go back to her son's house. And I refused blatantly. I have already made a vow to my creator in the hospital that I will never step a foot into his house again. After some weeks his mother now called me and my mother that she will do everything to get the custody of my two boys.

Then I called a friend who told me about DSVRT, domestic, sexual violence and rape team, I came to the office and met, with Madam Lola Vivour Adeniyi. She didn't just take up the case, she helped me heal. I was introduced to a psychologist who started therapy with me and given a lawyer to represent me in court. Before the court, He was called upon several times, and he refused to come and he kept on threatening and sending abusive messages.

I have been separated for three years, 10 months, almost 4 years now life as a single mother is a whole lot. But I am a survivor. It's been tough, hectic, painful and tiring but in all peaceful and full of life. I am living hopeful that all would be well someday. Majorly it's the shelter, feeding, upkeep of the children and education which is big deal but the burden has been so light weighted with the help of Mrs Lola Vivour Adeniyi, whom I call at every instance.

My six-year-old scared and jittery boy of yesterday life of abuse is now a very happy, peaceful and calm ten year old entering into JSS 1 and my 3 weeks baby of yesterday abuse is now 4 years about to start Nursery 2.

My advice to women that are still married to abusers is to speak up, seek help and stay alive. Thank you.

End

TRUE LIFE STORY

I got married in the year 1993. By God's grace, I have both girls and boys. I got married only to discover that I did not marry the love of my life. But married the mistake of my life. I got married to him when I was looking for who will stand in the gap of my father because I lost my father when I was young. In fact, I was told that I was born the very day my father was buried. So, I met my ex-husband after my secondary school, and he promised to send me to University if I would marry him, I was so happy that I will go to university.

After the marriage ceremony, things fell apart and the centre could not hold. Immediately I had my first daughter. I raised the issue of going back to school as he had promised. He said he just promised me that so that I would marry him. And that was when the problem started. Any time I reminded him of the promise he made, he will resort to slapping me.

Immediately my baby turned 6 months old, he told me that he wanted me to start trading. After contemplating on what I wanted to sell he arrived that he will tell our landlord to be giving me cement that after sales I will pay the balance.

So, he took me to the site where he worked because he is a welder engineer, he works on site building construction.

So, I started selling the cement and God being faithful, I had many customers.

From 15 bags of cement to 100 and so on. From the sales of cement, we bought land and he started building our own house gradually. I had another baby. That's how my life continued. Things got worse. I still continued. I can't complain to anybody because he did not allow anybody to move close to me. I don't have friends. In the church, I can't get close to anyone. One fateful day, he beat me and my uncle asked me what happened I told them and they talked to him but he never listened to my uncle. One time after he beat me, I ran to the nearby police station and the female officer advised me and gave me money to join with the little one I had with me to return to my hometown.

I ended up travelling only half way due to lack of money and it was late in the evening. On the road side while I was begging for money with my three kids, I saw a woman and I talked to her about my journey and she took me to Assemblies of God Church. After the midweek service, she took me to the pastor's wife. As I was narrating my story to the pastor, the pastor asked if I wanted to go back.

My first daughter said the pastor should not let me go back because her dad will kill me. So the second day the pastor gave me money and I went to my hometown but my mum said I should stay with the pastor wife immediately my husband and the relative come to look for me they will send someone to call me.

So, I went with the pastor and his wife to a nearby town along my hometown. There, I did different types of work to survive, such as following bricklayers to site to do decking by packing mixed cement to bricklayers, packing sand from a sand depot to resell, arranging block at site for bricklayers use, going to quarry to break stone (the granite stone). I did all of this just to survive and feed my children.

It was long holiday for my kids during the time I travelled. Unfortunately, the holiday was over and I was in that town. I started working with one nursery and primary school in that town (El-Shaddai Nursery and primary school), and my three kids were enrolled in the school.

I used my salary to pay for the school fees and I sold food stuff in small quantities. This was how I survived in that town. By the end of the first school session, I took my children to my hometown to spend the holidays. During that time, my husband and his relatives came and they were begging me to give my children to my husband who according to him, was no longer interested in me but as a family, they will talk to him. They appealed that I and the children should follow my husband back to Lagos. I felt like I had no choice and so I returned to Lagos with my children.

The struggle continued. Now in Lagos, my husband instructed that I should follow his sister to her house that he will come and meet us. When he finally come to meet us at his sister's house he said I should start living with his sister

I lived with his sister for two years. My husband never allows me to visit him. Rather, he comes any time he wishes. He refused to provide any feeding money or maintenance for me. His sister was gracious enough to help look for a job for me. I started working at Adunola Nursery and Primary school, Ebute Ikorodu.

Sometime in 2002, one fateful Sunday, my husband's relative came to meet me at the Pako (wood) house which the sister rented for me at Ipakodo Ebute and they took me and my three children to my husband.

I reunited once again with my husband and had two children. In year 2007, my last born became very sick and was diagnosed of sickle cell disorder, SSS genotype.

Immediately I returned to my husband's house I resumed the cement sale again because where I left the building, we were building is how I met it; uncompleted. So as I continued the sales of cement the building continued. Now I had many more customers than before. We finished the building, 8 flats 4 bedroom flats; 2 storey buildings located in Ikorodu.

Along the line, my baby with sickle cell was admitted at Ikorodu General Hospital, and my husband neglected me there. The doctor called him several times but he did not respond. The nurses assisted me by feeding me and my son.

In that very year, the maternity building in General Hospital Ikorodu was to be commissioned by Governor Fashola and the hospital needed more cleaners to join to make it fast so I left my son on the ward in care of other patients' relatives to assist and that was how I joined the cleaners. They paid us N500 (Five hundred naira) per day. I collected the money to buy food and drugs for me and my baby.

During that time they introduced me to Hon. Abike Dabiri Erewa. She gave me money and asked me to come to her office in Ikorodu in front of Oba Ayangburen's palace. She advised me and asked me to come with my certificate.

I went there with my secondary school results. I attended government College Ikorodu. Immediately I left the place, I took the letter to HEALTH SERVICE COMMISSION. I submitted the letter. When I was about to leave the hospital, I heard that the Lagos Teaching Hospital is looking for cleaners and so I went to LUTH that day and I submitted an application letter to work as a cleaner but thank God, I was called for an interview as a clerk.

I started working at LUTH in the year 2010. Now the beating and slapping increased because I told him that I want to work on my own. But God is faithful, I found favour. My son was doing fine and life continued. I managed my salary and I stopped depending on my husband since it is only if I ask for something, he will end up beating me. So, I stopped asking. The sexual abuses I experienced in his hands were very traumatic and when I refused his advances, he would start to blow me in areas there won't be any marks on my body.

In May 2018, my husband accused me of trying to kill him because according to him, he did not give me any of the rent from our building.

I remember going to the kitchen to get all the knives and keep them somewhere safe; unfortunately, I did not see any knife. I was so afraid to the extent that I could no longer sleep deep. My Blood Pressure rose to 192/180 and I was admitted.

After I was discharged, I made up my mind that I will not go home again so I stayed around the hospital premises. I started bathing in the public toilets and I would go to work from there.

After five days of being discharged from the hospital, I went home and took only my clothes and ran for my dear life. It was that time somebody introduce me to Sister Lola at DSVT, Domestic Sexual Violence Team. There, I introduced myself and narrated my story. At DSVT they introduced me to SME100. I was taught many things. How to be confident and move on with life. How to start my own business and make gain. How to forget the past and move on, not letting the past to control the future. After the training, I was given a certificate and a grant of ₦200,000.00 (Two hundred Thousand Naira).

My advice to women and men who are still experiencing this type of domestic violence is that they should speak up. The fear that people will be calling you different types of name such as (Asewo, Dalemosu, Oniranu, Failure etc.) should not dominate you. You have your life to live. Get out of that relationship that has no gain. Do not die there. Life continues. If you come out and pray and seriously focus, God will send help to you.

After I started my business with the money the Governor gave me, I was able to feed myself and my kids. Now, I have three graduates. My son that was diagnosed with sickle cell did not die. He is the HEAD BOY in his school, and he is doing fine.

My husband is really disappointed now. He is begging me to come and I said I can't come and die. I remember my husband made one statement at the welfare office in Ikorodu. Translating his comment from Yoruba to English, he said 'she will come back and beg, after all, this is not the first time she would leave because she can't live alone. Her head is in my armpit. I am in full control of her life.'

That means he thought there was no hope for me. But I am really appreciative of all that Sister Titilola and her team are doing for me. GOD BLESS THEM RICHLY. I'm alive today to share my story.

www.ingramcontent.com/pod-product-compliance
Lightning Source LLC
Chambersburg PA
CBHW041956260926
51850CB00022B/3432/J
* 9 7 8 5 3 8 2 2 1 8 6 1 8 *